101 DEFENSIVE BASKETBALL DRILLS

George Karl
Terry Stotts
Price Johnson

COACHES CHOICE

ISBN: 1-57167-079-3

Book Layout: Michelle Summers
Cover Design: Deborah M. Bellaire and Julie L. Denzer
Diagrams: Deborah M. Bellaire
Developmental Editor: Joanna Wright
Cover Photos: Courtesy of the NBA
          Front: Nathaniel S. Butler
          Back: Andy Hayt

Coaches Choice Books is an imprint of: Sagamore Publishing, Inc.
                                          P.O. Box 647
                                          Champaign, IL 61824-0647
                                          (217) 359-5940
                                          Fax: (217) 359-5975
                                          Web Site: http//www.sagamorepub.com

CONTENTS

ACKNOWLEDGMENTS

The authors would like to thank John Sullivan for his editorial assistance in helping to write up drills presented in this book. The authors are also grateful for the professional assistance in publishing this book provided by the staff of Coaches Choice Books and Videos—particularly Michelle Summers, Joanna Wright, Debbie Bellaire and Julie Denzer.

Finally, special thanks are extended to all of the players and coaches with whom we have had the opportunity to work with over the years. Their efforts and feedback have helped influence the design and ultimately the selection of the drills included in this book.

DEDICATION

This book is dedicated to our families—who motivated us to strive for excellence and reach for new heights. Their love enriches and energizes us.

George Karl
Terry Stotts
Price Johnson

PREFACE

For the more than three decades that I have been playing and coaching basketball, I have observed countless situations on the court and literally thousands of individuals attempting to play the game to the best of their abilities. Collectively, my experiences have given me an opportunity to evaluate many techniques and fundamentals for playing competitive basketball and a variety of methods for teaching those techniques and fundamentals. In the process, I have come to realize that true learning occurs when there is a need to know, a solid understanding of how to learn exists, and coaches and players realize that a particular goal can be reached.

My co-authors and I wrote this book to provide basketball coaches at all competitive levels with a tool that can enable them to maximize the skills and attributes of their players. As a vehicle for teaching and learning, properly designed drills can have extraordinary value. Each of the four volumes of drills in this series features drills that I have collected, court-tested, and applied over the course of my coaching career. If in the process of using the drills presented in this book coaches are better able to develop the skills of their players, then the effort to write these drill books will have been well worthwhile.

George Karl

DIAGRAM KEY

G   — guard

PG   — point guard

SG   —shooting guard

F   — forward

SF   —small forward

PF   — power forward

C   —center

———————————————→   —movement of a player

〜〜〜〜〜〜〜〜〜→   —movement of a player dribbling the basketball

———————————————┤   —movement of a player executing a screen

– – – – – – – – →   —movement of the basketball via a pass

CHAPTER 1

TRANSITION DRILLS

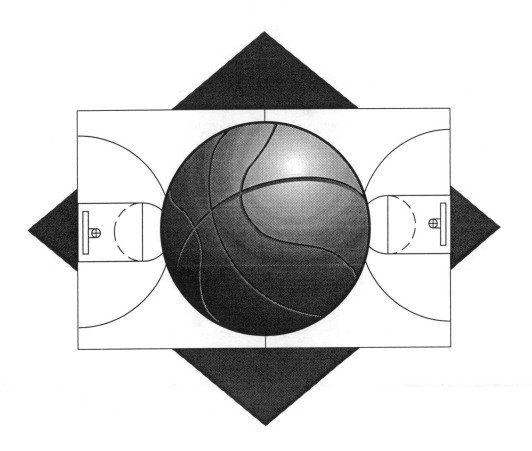

Drill #1: Safety First

Objective: To emphasize the importance of getting back on defense; to practice two-on-one defense.

Description: The coach should divide the squad into groups of four. The first group takes the court with two offensive players and two defensive players playing two-on-two around the foul line. The offensive player closest to the basket attempts to rebound and score, while his teammate retreats as a safety. When the defense gets the ball after a basket or on a rebound, they throw an outlet pass and sprint to fill the lane, creating a two-on-one situation. The player rebounding the ball makes no attempt to help, thereby leaving his teammate as the other defender alone to stop the two-on-one break. After a score or change of possession, the next group of four takes the court. The second time a group takes the court, the players reverse offensive and defensive roles. The drill should continue for two, four, or six rotations.

Coaching Points:

- The emphasis should be on the lone defender hurrying back and getting into proper position to stop the two-on-one break.
- The offensive players should practice executing the break properly.

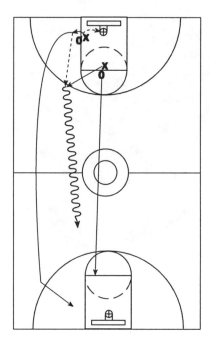

Drill #2: Three-On-Three With a Handicap

Objective: To practice transition defense when the offense has a temporary numerical advantage.

Description: The drill begins with three offensive and three defensive players positioned as shown in the diagram below. On the coach's signal, the middle defensive player slowly rolls the ball to the middle offensive player, then retreats to the safety position. The defender on the left wing drops back to the half-court line to attack the ball coming up the court. The three offensive players fill the lanes and push the ball up the floor, attempting to score in transition. The defender on the right wing must run forward and touch the baseline before sprinting down the court to aid his teammates, giving the offense a temporary advantage. After a score or change of possession, the teams reverse offensive and defensive roles and run the drill back down the court. The next group of six then takes the court. To add competition to the drill, the coach may decide to award points, for example, three to the defense for stopping a score, three to the offense for scoring before the third defender arrives to help, and two to the offense if the score is later. After the rotations have been completed, the winning team gets to watch the others run line drills.

Coaching Points:

- The emphasis should be placed on the safety getting quickly into proper position and the left wing defender challenging the ballhandler.
- The offense should practice filling the lanes and executing the break properly.

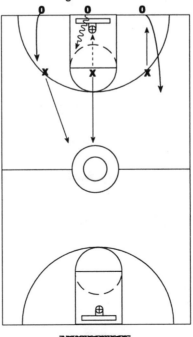

Drill #3: Five-On-Five Transition "D"

Objective: To practice transition defense in a turnover situation.

Description: The coach should divide the squad into two teams, rotating in extras to be sure all players participate. The drill begins with the two teams engaged in a half-court scrimmage. When the coach blows a whistle, whoever has the ball places it on the ground as if a turnover has just been created, and that player's team retreats into a defensive transition. The other team fills the lanes and moves downcourt, attempting to score as quickly as possible. The half-court scrimmage continues until the coach blows the whistle again, sending the action in the other direction.

Coaching Point:

- The coach should vary the location of the turnovers to provide practice for all types of transition defense.

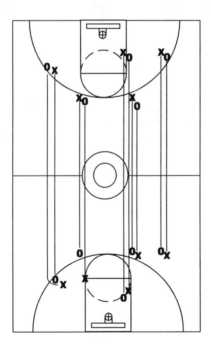

Drill #4: Beat Them to the Punch

Objective: To impress upon players the importance of being faster than their opponent when transitioning from offense into a pressing defensive scheme.

Description: This drill involves five-on-five competition. When a shot goes up, the first priority is playing for the offensive rebound. If the shot is made, the offense immediately switches into a pressing defensive scheme. The power forward (PF) beats the inbound passer to the baseline, and the shooting guard (SG) and small forward (SF) pick up the two opponents most likely to receive the inbound pass. The point guard (PG) retreats to the basket, and the center (C) hustles downcourt to assist. To conserve practice time, this drill may be stopped when the offense gets the ball over the mid-court line. The drill could also be expanded to practice the same full-court pressure after missed shots.

Coaching Point:

- The emphasis should be placed on beating the opposition to the punch. The PF should be waiting in position with his hands up for the inbounder to retrieve the ball.

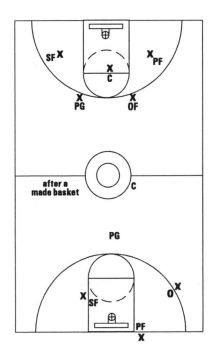

CHAPTER 2

MAN-TO-MAN DEFENSE DRILLS

Drill #5: Four-On-Four Around the Horn

Objective: To teach the basic fundamentals of keeping a proper defensive triangle position with emphasis on sagging and floating with ball movement.

Description: The coach should divide the team into groups of four. Two offensive guards and two wing players position themselves around the perimeter at the three-point line. Four defenders assume a good defensive position on their opponents. The offense passes the ball around the perimeter. In the early stages of the drill, the offense may only pass on a signal from the coach. They are not allowed to cut to the lane or make back-door moves, and no shot is taken. This stipulation allows the coach to make adjustments to the defensive players' reaction to a pass. As the drill progresses, the ball moves faster around the perimeter, requiring the defense to make the necessary adjustments.

Coaching Point:

- The coach should check each defender's position in relation to the ball, paying particular attention to making sure the guards sag enough to see the ball. Offside forwards should float when the ball is on the opposite side of the court.

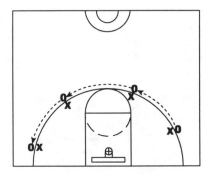

Drill #6: Make 'Em Change

Objective: To improve the defenders' ability to play good man-to-man defense against the dribble.

Description: The coach should divide the team into four equal groups. Two groups are on offense and are positioned single file on the baseline. Each offensive player should have a basketball. Two defensive players assume a good defensive stance, one in front of each offensive line. On the coach's command, the first two offensive players attempt to dribble downcourt as quickly as possible. The defenders attempt to alter the dribbler's course as often as possible between the baselines. The defenders may not use their hands, only good footwork and body positioning. The dribbler is limited to using half the width of the court to defeat the defender. When the first two groups reach the mid-court line, two more defenders assume their positions in front of the offensive lines, and the next two groups start downcourt.

Coaching Points:

- The coach may instruct the defenders to either keep their hands close to their sides, or use their hands in every way except stealing or deflecting the ball.
- The coach may also run the drill with three offensive lines, restricting the dribblers to one-third of the width of the court.

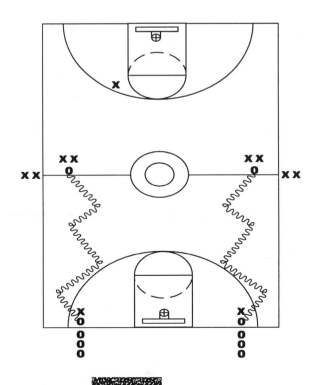

Drill #7: Protect the Lane Drill

Objective: To teach the proper sagging and floating techniques to defend against an opponent driving down the lane in a man-to-man defense.

Description: The coach should divide the squad into two teams. The offensive team runs a normal spread except for the point guard (PG), who is given a one-step advantage on his defender. On the coach's signal, PG drives the lane, attempting to score on a lay-up. The defensive team reacts accordingly, sagging and floating to prevent the lay-up. If PG is denied the lay-up, he should make the best pass available, forcing further defensive shifts. The drill may also be run with one of the forwards driving to the hoop from the corners.

Coaching Point:

• The coach should observe each player's position in relation to the ball and make adjustments where necessary.

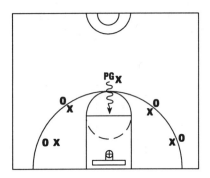

Diagram A

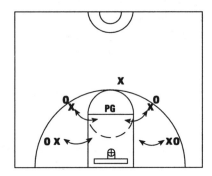

Diagram B

Drill #8: Trap With Your Feet

Objective: To improve the footwork and body positioning of players when they execute a double-team or two-man trap.

Description: The coach should divide the team into groups of three players. Each group should be stationed at a corner of the court. If more than four corners are necessary, use one or more of the corners created by the mid-court line. One player is positioned with a ball in the corner facing the center of the court. A defender is stationed three feet away, with a second defender directly behind the first. The offensive player attempts to dribble out either up the sideline or down the baseline. Using only footwork and body positioning, the first defender moves to cut off the dribbler's escape route. The second defender moves into position to execute a double-team trap, keeping the dribbler penned in the corner. The dribbler backs out of successful double-teams and keeps the dribble alive while continuously attempting to split or go around the trap.

Coaching Point:

• The defenders should allow the dribbler to back out of the double-team. When the coach decides to end the drill, a whistle can signal the defenders to become more aggressive and box the dribbler tightly in the corner.

Diagram A

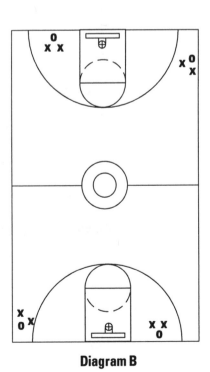

Diagram B

Drill #9: Help Against the Lob

Objective: To practice shifting and helping techniques against a lob into the post in a man-to-man defense.

Description: The coach should divide the squad into two teams. The drill begins with a full-speed half-court scrimmage. The offense's main objective is to get a lob pass in to the center (C). In the early stages of the drill, the offense runs a simple spread offense without cutting or screening. The defense's first objective is to deny the pass. Their second objective is to sag and rotate to disrupt C if he receives the pass and to rotate into possible passing lanes. The offside guard rotates to block the passing lane from C out to the forward. Offside forwards rotate to C, attempting to arrive just as he receives the lob.

Coaching Point:

- Each player's position in relation to the ball should be checked.

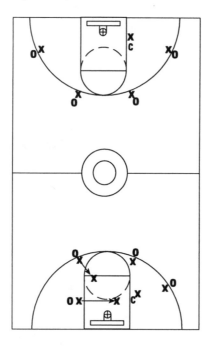

Drill #10: Low Post Five-On-One

Objective: To improve low post man-to-man defensive techniques with emphasis on footwork and body positioning.

Description: Four offensive players position themselves around the perimeter in the guard and wing positions. Another player is positioned as the center (C), assuming a strong stance with his arms extended. A single post defender takes a good three-quarter defensive stance, favoring the ballside shoulder. The offensive players pass the ball around the perimeter, looking for an opportunity to get the ball into C. C attempts to get open, and the defender uses quick footwork to maintain position. When the offense succeeds in getting the ball to C, he executes a variety of moves in an attempt to score.

Coaching Point:

- The coach should emphasize the quick footwork required of the low post defender, and stress the need to maintain contact at all times.

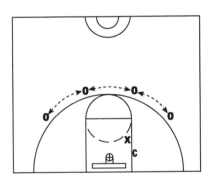

Drill #11: Body Keep Away

Objective: To improve man-to-man defensive skills by practicing the techniques necessary to successfully box out an opponent.

Description: The coach should divide the squad into pairs, one player on offense and the other on defense. The groups should be spaced in such a way to allow a six-foot circle for each pair to work in. A ball is placed in the center of the circle with the defender anywhere on the perimeter. The offensive player stands approximately one foot behind his opponent. The defender assumes a good block-out position with his feet moving quickly in position and his eyes looking for his opponent. The offensive player attempts to get to the ball. The defender uses his footwork and body position to keep his opponent away from the ball. The drill ends when the offensive player gets the ball or the coach blows the whistle again. Players should then switch roles and repeat the drill.

Coaching Points:

- The emphasis should be on the defenders keeping their hands raised and their elbows extended to create a bigger obstacle to the offensive player. The defenders should maintain a wide stance and keep their backs straight.
- Coaches may add competition to the drill by awarding points to the offensive players if they get to the ball within a specified amount of time or to the defensive players if they are successful in blocking out their opponent.

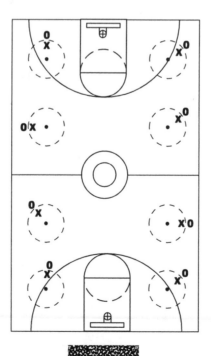

Drill #12: Draw the Foul Drill

Objective: To practice the basic fundamentals involved in correctly taking the charge.

Description: The coach should divide the team into groups of two players each, who take turns in the offensive and defensive roles. The players should line up facing each other ten to twelve feet apart, with the pairs well spaced. The offensive player simulates a drive to the hoop at half speed, and changes direction slightly as he penetrates. The defensive player should be in a good wide stance with his arms up and his back straight. He should use good quick footwork and lateral movement to get in proper position to take the charge. Using his hands or forearms, the offensive player knocks the defender to the ground. The defender scrambles up quickly. The players then change roles and continue.

Coaching Points:

- The coach should critique the defender's stance, footwork, and positioning. The emphasis should be placed on being set in time to draw the charge and on falling correctly.
- The tempo of the drill can be increased as players learn how to properly take the charge.

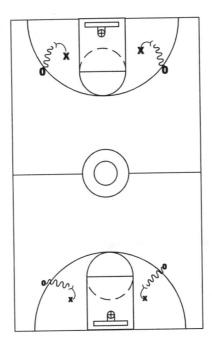

Drill #13: Deny the Center

Objective: To practice denying a pass from a guard or forward into the high or low post.

Description: This drill involves four players. A guard (G) and a post player (P) team up against two defenders. The guard attempts to pass into the high post area, and the defenders attempt to prevent it. The defensive guard should use proper footwork and keep his hands in the proper position while attempting to anticipate the pass. The post defender tries to force the center higher than he wants to go by pressuring the ballside shoulder. After defending the post from behind, the defender switches tactics and fronts his opponent. The drill can also be practiced between a forward and post player working the mid-to-low post area.

Coaching Point:

- There is a tendency during this drill for the defensive guard to sag more than he should to disrupt the pass. The coach should allow only proper game situation defensive fundamentals.

Drill #14: Drawing the Foul in the Lane

Objective: To practice the proper timing and techniques involved in taking a charge in the lane as an offensive player is driving to the hoop.

Description: The coach should divide the team into three equal groups positioned as shown in the diagram below. The first player in the first line has a basketball and acts as a guard (G). The players in the second line act as offensive forwards (F), while the third line should be made up of defenders (X). G passes the ball to F and makes a sharp cut to the basket. F passes back to G to complete the give and go. X has been guarding an imaginary man. When he sees the ball coming down the lane, he should move into position to draw the charge, taking care to be set before contact. X takes the charge and falls correctly. The next players in the lines begin the drill, continuing until all players have participated. Coaches may decide whether to have all players rotate into each line or separate them by position.

Coaching Points:

- The coach should emphasize proper footwork, body positioning, and being set in time to draw the charge.
- The defender should not switch off his imaginary man too soon, giving the guard time to change course or find an open pass.

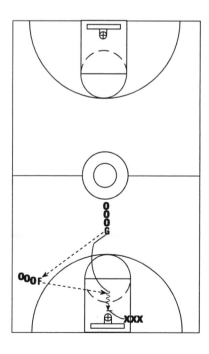

Drill #15: Clear Out "D"

Objective: To teach and practice various techniques used to defend against an opponent when offensive players clear out one side of the court in an attempt to get a one-on-one situation.

Description: This five-on-five drill begins with one offensive player and one defensive player on one side of the court in the wing position, and the other players on the other side of the court as shown in Diagram A. The one-on-one defender plays aggressive man-to-man defense, keeping the ballhandler from going to the middle and trying to force him to the baseline. As the ballhandler breaks to the middle or the baseline, the weakside defender nearest the ball slides over to help, and the other defenders rotate accordingly. If the ballhandler goes to the baseline, the defenders should double-team the ball. If the ballhandler gets to the middle, the nearest defender should pick him up, and the original defender should rotate to take over his teammate's responsibilities (Diagram B).

Coaching Points:

- The one-on-one defender should always try to force the ballhandler to the baseline so the most effective double-team can be used.
- The ballhandler should use different directions on the drive to practice different variations of help defense.

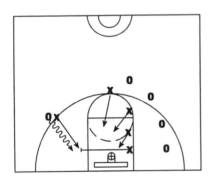

Diagram A

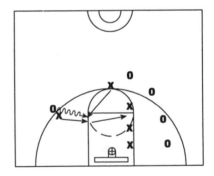

Diagram B

Drill #16: Five-On-Five Defensive Shift

Objective: To teach the proper defensive adjustments necessary in a man-to-man defense as the ball moves around the court on offense.

Description: The coach should divide the squad into two teams. The guards and forwards position themselves around the perimeter at the three-point line. The center is free to move around the post area at will. The defenders assume good defensive position on their opponents. The ball is passed around the perimeter or into the post. No pass can be made without a signal from the coach. No cutting into the lane or back-door moves are allowed, and no shot is taken. The coach should observe and make adjustments in the defenders' reaction to the ball position. As the drill progresses, the ball should move faster, requiring the defenders to make the proper shifts in defensive position. The coach may also decide to let the offense pass at will or use screens, cuts to the lane, or back-door moves.

Coaching Point:

- Each player's position in relation to the ball should be checked and corrected if necessary.

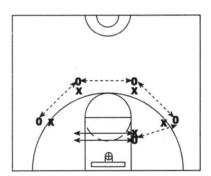

Drill #17: Ballside to Offside Cutters

Objective: To teach and practice the proper techniques used in defending against cutters going from the ballside to the offside of the court.

Description: This drill begins with the players positioned as shown in the diagram below. The point guard (PG) has the ball and attempts to pass to the forward (F) on the wing. The defender plays good man-to-man defense. When F drives to the baseline, his defender bumps F's ballside shoulder, then pivots and stays with him, keeping his body between F and the ball. The defender tries to beat F to the lane, forcing F to continue through the lane. The third defender is in the high deny position on the center (C). If F begins his cut from the ballside corner, his defender bumps the ballside shoulder and stays between F and the ball. The defender can remain in a help position on the weakside of the lane or return to the ballside to double-team the ball.

Coaching Point:

- Emphasize to defenders the importance of making the cutter go through, or around, their bodies. Defenders should not allow a cutter to get directly to a desired spot on the floor.

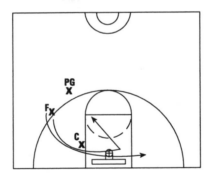

Drill #18: Drawing a Foul Off a Switch

Objective: To practice the proper timing and techniques in taking a charge while executing a switch off a screen.

Description: The coach should divide the team into three equal groups positioned as shown in the diagram below. The point guard (PG) has the ball and is guarded by an imaginary defender. As PG slides toward the side of the key, the shooting guard (SG) moves over to set a pick on the imaginary defender. The defensive player, who had been guarding SG, jumps into the path of PG to take the charge. Three new players move in, and the drill continues until the players have rotated through all three positions.

Coaching Point:

- The coach should emphasize proper footwork, body positioning, and being set in time to take the charge, as well as timing the move properly and falling correctly.

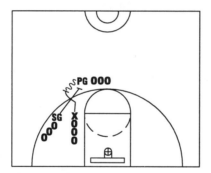

Drill #19: Offside to Ballside Cutters

Objective: To teach and practice the proper techniques in defending against cutters coming from the offside to the ballside of the court.

Description: This five-on-five drill begins with the players positioned as shown in Diagram A and the ball in the point guard's (PG) hands. The shooting guard (SG) executes a V-cut and attempts to get open down the lane. The defender bumps SG's ballside shoulder and turns down the lane, keeping his body between SG and the ball. The defender should not allow SG to get directly to his desired spot. He should make SG go through or around his body. Diagram B shows the drill with the power forward (PF) attempting to cut into the heart of the lane. PF's defender should be physical and force PF to go baseline. After forcing PF to go low, the defender should stay between PF and the ball and attempt to beat him to the spot of the pass. The small forward's (SF) defender should rotate down, and SG's defender should be alert for the pass to either SG or SF.

Coaching Point:

- The coach should emphasize to the defenders the importance of not allowing cutters to get directly to their desired spot on the floor.

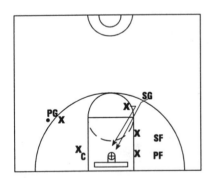

Diagram A

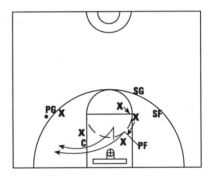

Diagram B

Drill #20: Deny and Help

Objective: To teach defenders how to make the transition from the denial position to the help position.

Description: This two-on-two drill involves an offensive guard (G) and a forward (F) and their defensive counterparts, positioned as shown in Diagram A. The guard dribbles toward F on the wing, and G's defender plays loose man-to-man defense, making no attempt to hinder the ballhandler. As G gets closer to F, F clears out to the weakside. F's defender denies the pass until F crosses the lane, then assumes a good help position and opens up so he can see both F and the ball. Diagram B shows the second defender in the help position as F moves back across the lane looking for a pass. The defender should beat F to the location to which the pass is most likely to be made. After a few repetitions, the players should rotate assignments. When the players have mastered the transition, G's defender should be allowed to play pressure defense, and the drill may be continued until there is a score or a change of possession.

Coaching Point:

- Emphasize the timing of when the defender switches between the denial and help positions.

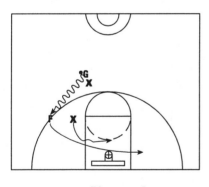

Diagram A

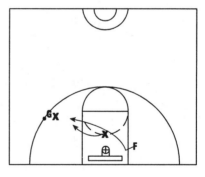

Diagram B

Drill #21: Help Against the Cut

Objective: To practice shifting and helping techniques in a man-to-man defensive scheme.

Description: The coach should divide the squad into two teams. The drill begins with a full-speed half-court scrimmage. The offensive team tries to use back-door moves and double cuts to get free from their defenders. The defensive players should communicate when they need help. Defenders should float and sag to cover their beaten teammates. The drill should be run long enough to ensure all players get both offensive and defensive practice. As players progress in their skills, the coach can introduce screens and double screens into the drill.

Coaching Points:

- The coach should pay special attention to the defensive shifts and stop the scrimmage to make corrections when necessary.
- Defensive communication should be emphasized.

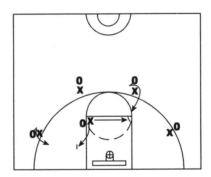

CHAPTER 3

FOOTWORK DRILLS

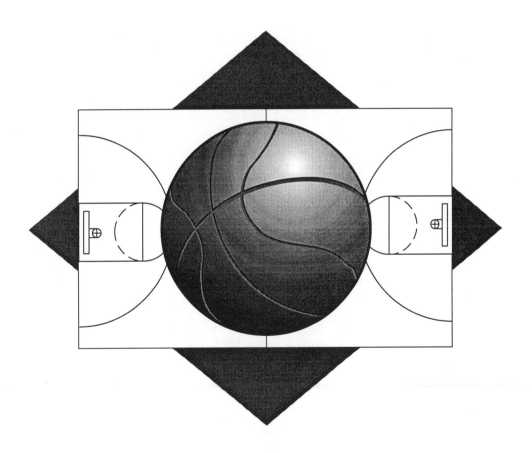

Drill #22: Slow "Mo"

Objective: To teach and reinforce the elements of proper footwork, to develop stamina and leg conditioning.

Description: This drill should be used early in the season after the coach has taught the preferred stance and footwork techniques. The squad should be divided into three rows with the players evenly spaced. The player at the right end of each line should begin at the left sideline. The players assume a good defensive stance, and, on the coach's command, slide slowly across the court to the opposite sideline. When the players at the right ends of the rows reach the right sideline, they shout reverse, and the rows slide slowly in the other direction. The players should perform the movements slowly and exaggerate proper technique.

Coaching Point:

- The coach should gradually increase the length of time the drill is performed as conditioning levels increase.

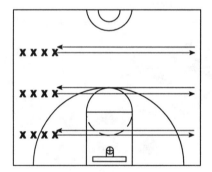

Drill #23: No Hands

Objective: To improve proper defensive technique by eliminating the use of the hands so players can concentrate on their footwork.

Description: This drill should be used early in the season after the coach has taught the preferred stance and footwork techniques. The players should be spaced evenly on the court so each has room to maneuver. Each player holds a towel under his neck to force him to concentrate on his footwork. On the coach's command, the players slide from side to side and shuffle forward and back. After a minute or two, the coach should divide the team into two groups. Half the team forms a line at an offensive wing position. The rest of the players become defenders and form a line behind the baseline, still holding their towels. The first defender assumes a defensive wing position, and the first offensive player is given a ball. He makes a move to drive the lane or go baseline. The defender attempts to prevent penetration. Once again, the towel forces the defender to use footwork to get his body in position to cut off the drive.

Coaching Point:

- Coaches can eliminate the towel and require players to keep their arms down at their sides.

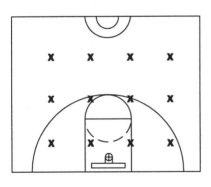

Diagram A

Diagram B

Drill #24: Baseline-to-Baseline Drill

Objective: To improve the ability to maintian proper defensive body position and use proper footwork ; to develop leg strength and stamina.

Description: The players form a line on one baseline in a good defensive position. On the coach's command, the players move forward, back, left, and right down the court. They should keep their back to the baseline from which they started and never raise out of a good defensive stance. At least twice during the trip downcourt, the coach should shout "change." At this command, the players should switch so that their other foot is in the forward position. When they reach the other baseline, the players should make a 180-degree turn without raising out of a good defensive position.

Coaching Points:

- The coach should observe the players' body position and footwork and critique where necessary without stopping the drill.
- The number of trips the players make up and down the court should be increased periodically to further improve stamina and leg strength.

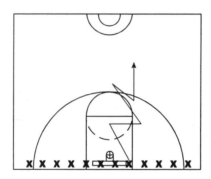

Drill #25: Observe and React

Objective: To improve defensive body position and perfect the techniques used in the sliding step.

Description: The coach should divide the team into two groups that will operate independently on opposite ends of the court. One player from each group serves as a common opponent for the other members of his group. Both groups start near midcourt, centered between the sidelines with their backs to the baseline. The offensive players move forward, sideways, and backward, gradually working toward the baseline. They should try to force as many changes in defensive position and footwork as possible. The defenders should learn to react and change positions correctly. On reaching the baseline, the offensive player switches roles with one of the defenders, and the players hustle to midcourt to repeat the drill.

Coaching Points:

- If two coaches are available, one should work with each group. If not, the coach should rotate between the groups, making corrections where necessary.
- Once the fundamentals of the crossover step have been taught, it can be integrated into this drill.

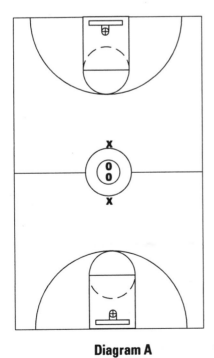

Diagram A

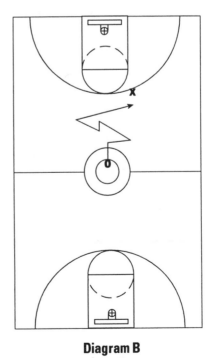

Diagram B

Drill #26: Held Together By a Thread

Objective: To improve a defensive player's body position, footwork, and reaction time.

Description: The coach should divide the team into groups of two. The drill begins at one baseline and ends at the other. Only one pair starts at a time. When that pair of players reaches the midcourt line, the next two players begin. The offensive player is linked to his defender by a five-foot string, tied loosely to belts worn by each player. The defender assumes a good defensive position, and reacts to the offensive player's maneuvers downcourt. The offensive player changes direction frequently, trying to break the string. This action forces the defender to react quickly and maintain good body position through proper footwork. The offensive player may use the entire width of the court.

Coaching Points:

- Coaches should make corrections on technique where necessary.
- The coach may choose to run the drill at half-speed initially, gradually increasing the speed of the drill. The string can be shortened to increase the difficulty of the drill.

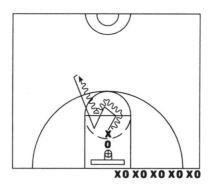

Drill #27: Forward and Back and Slide to Slide

Objective: To improve footwork techniques used to go forward, back, left, and right; to improve conditioning levels.

Description: The coach splits the team into two groups, one working at each end of the court. The players form a line outside the baseline under the basket. The first player assumes a good defensive stance and shuffles forward to the free-throw line, keeping one hand up and one hand down to help maintain his balance. He then slides to the right sideline. He should use a slide step only, never a crossover, and concentrate on proper technique. The player proceeds around the court as shown in the diagram below, shuffling forward or back and sliding left or right as needed. The player then returns to the end of the line and repeats the same process until the coach ends the drill.

Coaching Point:

- The coach may choose to start other players through the drill as the first player reaches the free-throw line. This action will increase the conditioning aspect of the drill. If the coach wants to observe the players' technique more closely, he would start players farther apart.

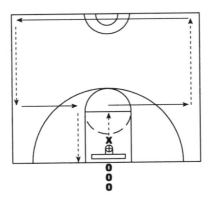

Drill #28: Controlled One-on-One

Objective: To improve a player's defensive body position and footwork skills while working against a dribbler.

Description: Two players participate in this drill at a time. One is on offense moving the ball down the court and the other is defending against the dribble. The offensive player may utilize half the width of the court. He may use crossover dribbles, reverse spins, and drop step techniques, but he should not try to beat the defender. The focus of this drill is on the defender's techniques and footwork. He should stay close enough to touch the dribbler, and keep his head between the ball and the basket. Using the hand nearest the direction the ball is moving, the defender tries to knock the ball away. The coach may watch the pair the entire length of the court or start the next pair as the first players pass half-court.

Coaching Points:

- The coach should be sure players pivot and execute the slide steps properly. Players should never cross their feet when moving or changing directions.
- Although the primary focus of this drill is on defense, the offensive players get practice protecting the ball.

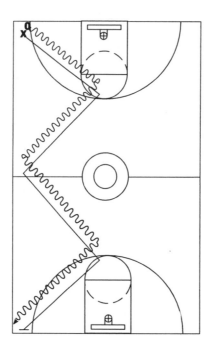

Drill #28: Shuffle and Slide Conditioning

Objective: To improve players' shuffle and slide step proficiency; to increase conditioning levels.

Description: The players should form a line along one sideline of the court. On the coach's command, the players, in good defensive position, slide step to the other sideline and back. When they return to the starting point, they turn to face the opposite line, then shuffle step across the court. On the return trip, they execute a backward zig-zag slide and pivot movement. The duration of the drill depends on the conditioning level of the players. As the season progresses, the coach should increase the length of the drill. Players should not be allowed to stand up straight or rest during the drill.

Coaching Point:

- The coach should make certain all players remain in a good defensive position throughout the drill. When sliding, the players' palms should be up. When shuffling, one hand should be up and one hand down to maintain balance.

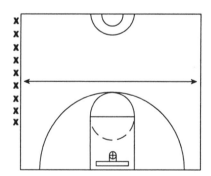

Drill #30: Put It In Reverse

Objective: To teach proper fundamentals of changing directions while backing up in a defensive position; to improve leg strength and endurance.

Description: The coach divides the team into groups of four, which line up on one baseline facing out of bounds. The first player in each group assumes a good defensive stance, and, on the coach's signal, begins retreating against an imaginary ballhandler, focusing on the coach's hand. The players first slide to their right. After a few slide steps, the coach signals with his hand to pivot and start retreating in the other direction. Players plant their rear foot and pivot, keeping their bodies open to the imaginary ballhandler. They continue down the floor in a zig-zag pattern. When the first group makes its second pivot, the next group of players starts downcourt.

Coaching Point:

- Coaches may run this drill slowly, stopping to make corrections, or increase the speed to emphasize tbe conditioning aspects of the drill.

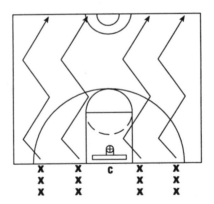

CHAPTER 4

ZONE DEFENSE DRILLS

Drill #31: Defending the Baseline Screen

Objective: To teach defenders in a zone the proper techniques involved in avoiding screening maneuvers.

Description: This drill involves three offensive players and three defenders, positioned as shown in the diagram below. The guard (G) begins the drill with the ball. The center (C) sets a baseline screen, attempting to spring the forward (F) free for a short jump-shot. G passes to F for the shot, and G's defender offers only token defense. The defenders guarding F and C either switch or fight over the top of the screen to deny the shot. The defenders should use whichever maneuvers the coach prefers. If F does not get the shot, C moves to the other side of the lane, and the ball is returned to G. The drill should continue until all players who might see action at the baseline defensive positions have rotated in.

Coaching Points:

- The coach should adapt this drill to suit the zone defense his team plays.
- Although the primary focus of this drill is on defense, it offers an opportunity for the coach to instruct the offensive players on how to attack the zone with screens.

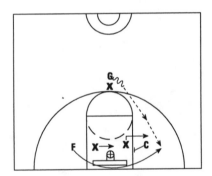

Drill #32: Post Reaction Drill

Objective: To improve the reaction time and body positioning skills of players defending the pivot area in a zone defense.

Description: The coach selects six players to play offense against a lone defender. The defender is located in the low post area as he would be in a zone defense. The offensive players are positioned as shown in the diagram below, with the three pairs designated A, B, and C. The coach passes to one of the offensive players. If the ball goes to either of the B players, the second B makes a sharp cut and breaks into the pivot area. His teammate attempts to pass the ball in to him, and the defender tries to deny the pass. If the pass is successful, the two players go one-on-one until a basket is made or the ball changes possession. The coach puts the second ball in play immediately after the one-on-one game is over to keep the drill moving and pressure the defender to react quickly.

Coaching Point:

- The coach should stress correct body position and keeping the hands in the air and emphasize beating the offensive player to the spot where he would like to receive the pass.

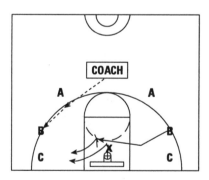

Drill #33: Rebound and Go

Objective: To improve players' skills in establishing proper rebounding position in a zone defense; to practice the beginning of a transition break.

Description: This drill involves five offensive players against five defensive players, who are aligned in whichever zone the coach desires. The offense consists of three perimeter and two baseline or post players. One of the forwards (F) passes to the point guard (PG), who puts up a quick shot. The defenders should block out a player or protect an area, depending on what is appropriate. To pressure the defenders, all five offensive players should crash the boards. On offensive rebounds, play continues with the rebounder attempting to score. On a defensive rebound, the rebounder makes a quick outlet pass to start the break. Players fill the lanes in transition, but stop the drill at half-court to set up the drill again. The drill should continue until all players have rotated in on defense.

Coaching Point:

- As skill levels increase, the coach should change the drill to allow more passes and vary the location of the shots.

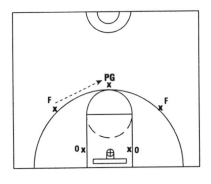

Diagram A

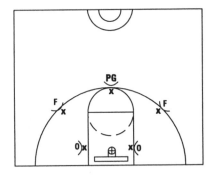

Diagram B

Drill #34: Rotate and Trap Drill

Objective: To teach players the proper rotation in a zone defense when an offensive player has successfully driven the baseline.

Description: In this five-on-five drill, the coach should position the defenders in a 2-3 zone and the offensive players as shown in the diagram below. The point guard (PG) has the ball and may pass to either the shooting guard (SG) or small forward (SF). In the illustration below, PG passes to SF, whose first choice is to beat his defender on a baseline drive. If he cannot, he may pass back to PG, cross court to the power forward (PF), or into the center (C). All of these actions require quick responses from the defenders, who must slide to their designated areas to cut off the pass from SF. If SF is able to beat his defender on the baseline, the post defender moves over to trap with the original defender, and the other defenders should react accordingly. This drill should be run for an extended period of time to be sure all players get in on the defensive action.

Coaching Point:

- The coach should not hesitate to stop this drill to make corrections in the rotation. As fundamentals improve, the drill can be expanded by allowing any offensive player to pass to any teammate or to drive the lane.

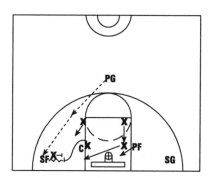

Drill #35: Five-On-Five Cut

Objective: To improve a defender's ability to defend against cutters in a zone defense.

Description: This drill involves five offensive players against five defenders who are aligned in whichever zone defense the coach desires. The point guard (PG) and the ballside forward (F) pass the ball back and forth looking for an opportunity to pass inside to any of the other three offensive players. Any of the weakside players may cut to the lane to receive a pass. Defenders sag and slide according to their responsibilities in an attempt to deny the pass. If the cutter receives the pass, he should attempt to score. The drill continues in a half-court scrimmage style with the offense and defense switching on a score or change of possession. The coach should make sure all players get to rotate into the drill.

Coaching Point:

- The coach may choose to have the offense use weakside screens as the skill levels progress.

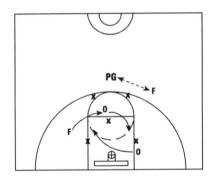

Drill #36: Cover the Cutter

Objective: To improve defensive communication and shifting techniques in a zone defense against players cutting to the lane.

Description: This drill involves four offensive and four defensive players—two guards and two forwards. The center does not participate. The players are positioned as shown in the diagram below. The point guard (PG) passes to the small forward (SF) and cuts through the lane looking for a return pass. All defenders slide and sag as indicated in the diagram to rotate into position to continue coverage. If the defender nearest PG decides to follow the cut, he must communicate verbally with his teammates so they can rotate properly. The offensive players may pass and cut or just pass. The offense should emphasize ball movement to keep the defenders adjusting and thinking quickly.

Coaching Points:

- The coach should adapt this drill to suit the zone(s) his team plays.
- This drill also gives offensive players an opportunity to practice perimeter passing and passing the ball inside against a zone defense.

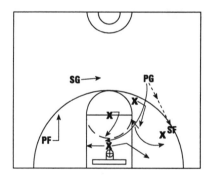

Drill #37: Defending the Corner

Objective: To teach players to trap in the corner and play the passing lanes in a zone defense.

Description: This four-on-four drill uses only one side of the offense at a time. Players should position themselves as shown in the diagram below. The ball begins with the shooting guard (SG), who passes in the corner to the small forward (SF). SF may pass back to SG or over to the power forward (PF). Any ball movement forces the defense to rotate into the passing lanes and disrupt the offensive flow. When the ball goes to the corner, the defender nearest SG decides whether to play the lane or execute a trap on SF with his teammate. The other defensive players adjust according to his decision. If the trap is set, the defender nearest the point guard (PG) must choose whether to guard SG, play the passing lane between SG and the power forward (PF), or guard PF. This drill should be run on both sides of the lane.

Coaching Points:

- The coach should be sure all fundamentals of zone defense are played correctly, and should stop the drill if necessary to make corrections.
- This drill also allows the coach to teach the offensive players how to pass against a zone defense that emphasizes trapping and playing the passing lanes.

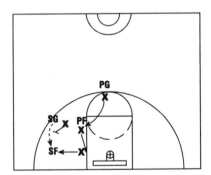

Drill #38: React and Adjust

Objective: To improve defenders' ability to react and adjust to their responsibilities in a zone defense.

Description: This drill involves six offensive players against five defenders, who are aligned in any zone defense the coach desires. The offense consists of two baseline and four perimeter players. At the beginning of the drill, the offensive players are restricted to their own areas. The goal of the offense is rapid ball movement around the perimeter, into the post, and back out. This action forces the defenders to sag and slide according to their individual responsibilities. In the initial teaching stages, the coach may wish to have the offensive players hold the ball until the defenders have adjusted, providing an opportunity for corrections. As players become more familiar with their responsibilities, the speed of the drill should increase. The drill should continue until all players have rotated in on defense. The drill may also be run with three offensive players on the perimeter and three in the post, or with three perimeter players, two post players, and a baseline runner.

Coaching Point:

- As skill levels increase, the coach may decide to allow screening and cutting by the offense.

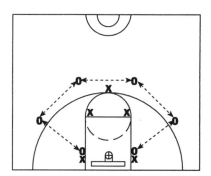

Drill #39: Give 'Em Only What You Want

Objective: To teach defenders in a zone how to keep the ball in a particular area of the floor.

Description: This drill involves five offensive players and four defenders. Players should position themselves as shown in the diagram below. In this drill, the center (C) remains stationary throughout the drill. His only role is to receive and make passes. The drill begins with the point guard (PG) with the ball. The defender nearest PG should overplay him to the right, and the defender nearest the small forward (SF) should play the passing lane between PG and SF. The defender on the opposite wing has sagged off the shooting guard (SG), giving PG the easy pass to SG. When SG receives the pass, the defenders slide into the passing lanes as shown in the diagram below. This effectively denies SG the opportunity to pass to anyone but C. Defenders continue to adjust to deny the passing lanes in an effort to keep the ball on the right side of the court.

Coaching Point:

* This drill may be run in other areas of the court to force opponents to put the ball in the hands of the player or area the coach feels is most vulnerable.

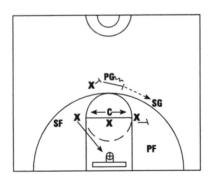

Drill #40: Preventing the Drive

Objective: To teach defenders in a zone defense the proper techniques involved in stopping a dribbler's penetration down the lane.

Description: This drill involves three offensive players and either three or five defensive players. In the three-on-three version of the drill, players should position themselves as shown in the diagram below. In the five-on-five version, two additional defenders play the low post positions. The drill begins with the ball in the guard's (G) hands. He can pass to either of the forwards (F) or drive down the lane. If he drives the lane, the wing defenders sag and help as indicated in the diagram, being prepared to quickly recover to their own area. If one of the forwards receives a pass from G, he may pass back to G or drive to the lane to try to get an open jump-shot. If the defenders sag properly, F's only option will be to pass back out to G.

Coaching Point:

- This drill can be adapted to emphasize a coach's particular philosophy of zone defense. It can also be adapted to cover dribbling penetration from each defender's area of responsibility.

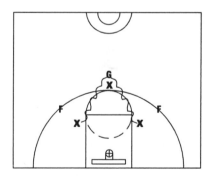

Drill #41: Five-On-Five Drive

Objective: To improve a defender's ability to react and adjust against a dribbler's penetration in a zone defense.

Description: This drill involves five offensive players and five defensive players who are aligned in any zone defense the coach desires. The five offensive players are positioned around the lane on the perimeter. They pass the ball around the perimeter to force the defense to sag and slide. When any of the offensive players sees an opening, he may drive to the lane, and either pass or shoot. No shots are taken from the perimeter. The offense must drive on every possession. The offense and defense switch roles on a change of possession or a score. This drill may also be run with a high and low post or a double post, leaving only three perimeter players. The perimeter players must still drive on every possession.

Coaching Point:

- The coach should make sure all of the rules regarding sagging and sliding are followed. He should not hesitate to stop the drill to make corrections.

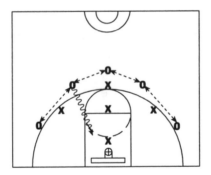

Drill #42: Defending the Perimeter Screen

Objective: To teach defenders in a zone defense the proper techniques involved in avoiding screening maneuvers.

Description: This drill involves three offensive players and three defenders, positioned as shown in the diagram below. The point guard (PG) begins the drill by dribbling toward the small forward (SF). The shooting guard (SG) moves to the top of the key to fill PG's position as SF sets a screen for PG. The defender guarding PG fights over or around the screen or switches with the defender guarding SF, depending on the coach's rules. After screening, SF moves cross court to fill SG's position. The offensive players can drive or shoot at any time. Defenders must block out on the shot and sag or slide into position to help on the drive. The drill should continue until all perimeter players have rotated in on defense.

Coaching Points:

- The coach should adapt this drill to suit the zone defense(s) his team plays.
- This coach may also use this drill to teach the offense how to attack a zone by using screens.

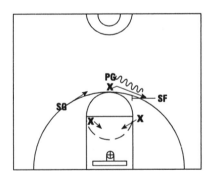

CHAPTER 5

FULL-COURT DEFENSE DRILLS

Drill #43: Full-Court Two-on-Two

Objective: To improve a defender's full-court defensive skills by practicing denying the inbound pass; to practice applying full-court man-to-man pressure.

Description: This drill involves four players at a time, two on offense and two on defense, positioned as shown in the diagram below. The man guarding the inbounder should play as close to the inbounder as allowed and do everything possible to distract and harass him. The other defender plays the passing lane, remaining in a position to see his man and the ball at all times. He attempts to deny his man access to the lane and force him to the baseline. If the ball is inbounded successfully, the inbounder cuts in front of his teammate for a return pass. The other offensive player either makes the pass or moves the ball up the court. The defenders should play pressure defense in either case. Play continues until there is a score or change of possession at the far end of the court. The players reverse offensive and defensive roles and run the drill in the other direction. The offense should continue attempting to inbound the ball until they are successful. When the first group of players has returned to the starting point, the next group begins. The drill can also be shortened by dividing the groups between the two baskets and stopping the action at half-court.

Coaching Points:

- The emphasis should be placed on forcing the receiver to the baseline. This angle is the most difficult one for inbounding the ball. If the ball is inbounded successfully, the offensive player may be trapped in the corner.
- The coach should stress the importance of denying the passing lane.

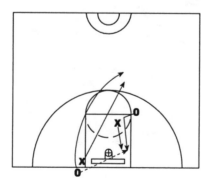

Drill #44: Side-to-Side Zig-Zag

Objective: To improve a defender's agility and coordination while moving side-to-side in a zone press.

Description: The coach should divide the team into three groups, which form three lines outside the baseline as shown in the diagram below. The first player in each line assumes a defensive position. The next player in each line is given a ball to throw a long inbound pass. On the coach's signal, the defenders retreat quickly at an angle. After a few steps, they pivot, always facing the ball, and retreat in the other direction. The defenders should never take their eyes off the ball or turn their backs to it. When they have zig-zagged their way to half-court, the inbounders throw a baseball pass downcourt. The pass should be difficult, but not impossible, to intercept. The defenders then throw a baseball pass back to the next player in each line and the inbounders become the defenders. The original defenders go to the end of their respective lines.

Coaching Point:

- Although the drill focues on defense, it also provides players the opportunity to practice using a baseball pass to inbound the ball.

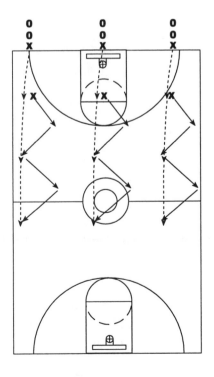

Drill #45: Score and Steal

Objective: To practice stealing a pass in a zone press; to practice setting up the press quickly after a score.

Description: This drill involves five defenders and one inbound passer, and can be adapted to any zone the coach wishes to teach. The defenders run an offensive play and any one of the players puts up a shot. If the shot misses, three players crash the boards, while the other two position themselves as safeties. When the first or follow-up shot goes in, the players scramble to their defensive assignments. The low post defenders then retreat to mid-court to discourage the lob, while the high post defenders protect their areas against the inbound pass. The defender in the lane sprints down the court to help on long passes. As soon as the shot is made, the inbounder grabs the ball and makes a soft lob pass to a vacant area. The defenders react and adjust accordingly. The drill is repeated until everyone has rotated in on defense.

Coaching Point:

- The coach should have the players who usually inbound the ball to perform that duty in this drill. As the drill progresses, the inbound pass can be made more difficult to defense.

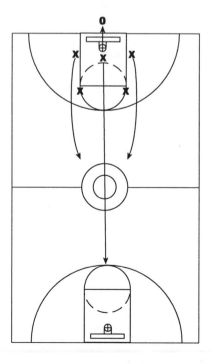

Drill #46: Fullcourt Three-on-Three

Objective: To improve a defender's ability to deny the inbound pass; to practice applying full court man-to-man pressure.

Description: This drill involves three offensive and three defensive players, positioned as shown in the diagram below. The defensive player guarding the inbounder should harass and distract the inbounder as much as possible. The offensive player above the free-throw line cuts first. If he is not able to receive the pass, the other offensive player cuts in the opposite direction. If the offensive players screen for each other, the defenders must stay with their men; no switching is allowed in the drill. If the inbound pass is successful, the defenders apply fullcourt pressure defense, attempting to turn the dribbler as often as possible and deny the pass. The drill continues downcourt until a score or change of possession. Players then reverse offensive and defensive roles and run the drill in the opposite direction. When they return to the original starting point, the next group begins. The drill can also be run only to half-court, allowing two groups to participate at a time.

Coaching Point:

- This drill may be modified to fit any inbound scheme an opponent might run.

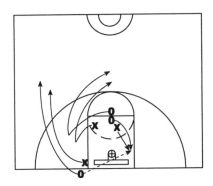

Drill #47: Easing Into the Full-Court Press

Objective: To teach players their basic responsibilities in full-court press schemes; to improve players' ability to defend the passing lanes.

Description: In this five-on-five drill, the coach sets up the offense in an inbound alignment and positions the defenders accordingly. While the coach is teaching, no pass should be made except on his command. The coach dictates where and when the next pass will be made. After the pass is made, the offense remains in place, allowing the defenders to learn the passing lanes and their responsibilities. Once the defenders have a clear understanding of their duties, the coach can allow the offense to move and pass on their own. This drill may be run in place, at half-speed, or at full-speed, depending on the skill levels of the players.

Coaching Point:

- The coach should vary the offensive inbound alignment to prepare the defenders for different situations.

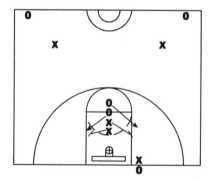

Drill #48: Overload Four-On-Three

Objective: To teach and practice the proper way to handle a situation where the offense has a numerical advantage.

Description: Four offensive players should set up at midcourt and work against three defenders positioned in a triangle zone. The offense should try to make the most of their numerical advantage and score quickly. The defense tries to delay the action by forcing as many passes as possible. The defenders should sag and guard against cutters to prevent a lay-up. To emphasize to the offense the importance of scoring quickly, a fourth defender may be positioned at midcourt. When play begins, he must run to the opposite free-throw line before rushing downcourt to help his teammates.

Coaching Point:

- The emphasis should be on forcing the first pass and then quickly rotating the zone to force the next pass.

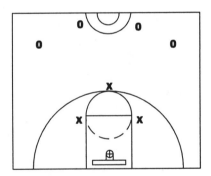

Drill #49: Fullcourt Four-on-Four

Objective: To improve a defender's ability to deny the inbound pass; to practice applying full court man-to-man pressure.

Description: Four offensive players and four defenders are positioned as shown in the diagram below. The defender guarding the inbounder should do everything possible to distract him. The defender at the free-throw line should be in position to see both his man and the ball while playing the passing lane. He should deny his man access to the lane and try to force him toward the baseline. The other two defenders should be ready to help on a lob pass. If the inbound pass is successful, all defenders apply full-court pressure, attempting to turn the dribble as often as possible and deny the pass. Play continues until a score or change of possession. The defenders switch roles with their offensive counterparts on the next rotation of the drill.

Coaching Point:

- Defenders should not be allowed to switch during this drill. The emphasis should be placed on communication and fighting through any screens set by the offense.

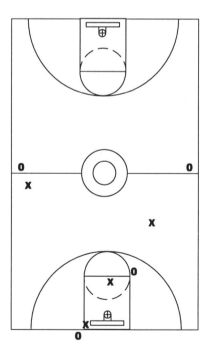

Drill #50: Trapping In the Zone Press

Objective: To teach the double-team trap, the areas of responsibility, and the passing lanes in the zone press.

Description: Seven offensive players and five defensive players are positioned as shown in the diagram below. The point guard (PG) dribbles the ball as if he had received the inbound pass. The two defenders nearest PG set up a double team trap and try to force PG to pick up the dribble before he can pass. PG may pass to any of the other three players in the back court. The other two defenders in the back court try to react and intercept PG's pass. If the pass is successful, the receiver looks to the offensive players in the front court to complete the breaking of the press. The single front-court defender splits the area among the three, trying to anticipate and steal the pass. If he attempts to intercept the pass, he should be sure of the steal. If he is not certain of the steal, he should retreat into the safety position.

Coaching Point:

- This drill may be altered to practice trapping anywhere on the court.
- It should be emphasized to defenders to play between the offensive players in the defenders' area of responsibility.

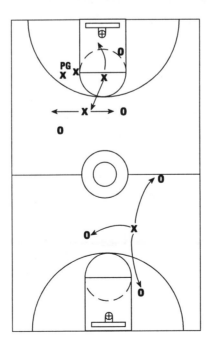

Drill #51: Score and Press

Objective: To teach players to react quickly and get to their areas of responsibility after a score.

Description: This drill involves five offensive and five defensive players. The offense takes the ball out at half-court and attempts to score. They are given 15 seconds to work for a shot. If they are unable to get a shot off, the defense is awarded three points, and the offense must try again. When a shot goes up, all the offensive players should crash the boards. In this drill, the defense is not allowed to fast break. If the defense controls the rebound, they earn a point. If the offense scores, they get two points. On a score, defensive rebound, or change of possession, the defensive team quickly attempts an inbound pass. The shooting team should react quickly and move to their pressing assignments. The new defensive team may earn three points for stealing or deflecting the inbound pass or creating a turnover before the ball gets to half-court. When the new offensive team reaches half-court, they have 15 seconds to score. Scoring is weighted in favor of defensive performance.

Coaching Points:

- The emphasis should be placed on harassing the inbound pass, playing the passing lanes, and forcing the dribbler to alter his course.
- Offensive players should be sure to crash the boards and avoid the tendency to rush to their pressing positions before a rebound is secured.

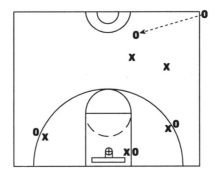

Drill #52: Five-on-Five Pressure "D"

Objective: To improve a defender's full-court pressure defense.

Description: Two five-player teams should be positioned as shown in the diagram below. The defensive player guarding the inbounder does his best to distract and harass the inbounder. The defender near the free-throw line denies his man access to the lane and tries to force him toward the baseline. The defenders guarding the men at half-court should be prepared to deny the lob pass. The final defender should be ready to help on the lob pass and also keep his man from breaking to midcourt to receive a pass. Play continues until a score or change of possession.

Coaching Point:

- The coach should adapt this drill to practice against various inbound alignments.

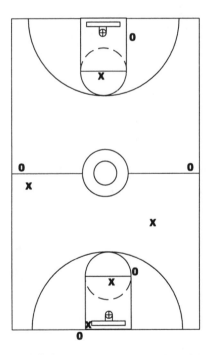

Drill #53: Overload Three-On-Two

Objective: To teach and practice the proper way of handling a situation where the offensive team has a three-on-two advantage.

Description: Five players, three on offense and two on defense, should stand even with one free-throw line and face the opposite basket. On the coach's signal, the defensive players race downcourt, as if retreating on a break situation. The coach then chooses when to give the offensive players the signal to break. The defenders establish a good tandem position. They attempt to force as many passes as possible and give up nothing but a jump-shot. This drill may also be run three-on-three by delaying the start of the third defender, thereby placing emphasis on forcing enough passes for the third defender to catch up.

Coaching Point:

- When teaching the tandem defense, the coach should give the defenders time to get down the court and set up. As skill levels increase, the offensive players should be released sooner to apply more pressure and force quicker decisions.

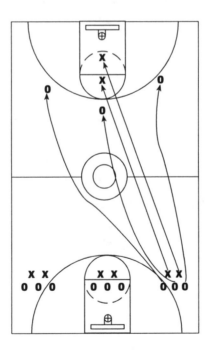

CHAPTER 6

ONE-ON-ONE DRILLS

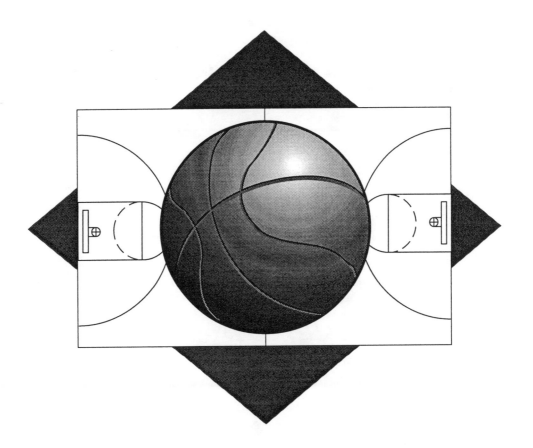

Drill #54: One-On-One Plus

Objective: To teach defenders their responsibilities when playing pressure defense.

Description: This drill begins with a point guard (PG) at the top of the key and an offensive player and defensive player positioned as shown in the diagram below. PG is not defended, as he is only there to aid the other offensive player. On a signal from PG, the offensive player cuts backdoor through the lane. The defender, who had been overplaying his opponent, pivots through the lane to deny the backdoor pass. PG makes the pass if it is open. If it is not, the offensive player continues through the lane to the opposite wing while PG dribbles down to the wing area vacated by the other two players. The offensive player then breaks to the lane for a pass, and the defender tries to deny it. The offensive player then breaks down the lane. The defender must react quickly to stay between his opponent and the ball. PG may pass or drive to the hoop at any time to make sure the defender is alert.

Coaching Point:

- The emphasis should be placed on proper defensive footwork and pivots, as well as constant eye contact with the ball.

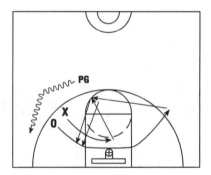

Drill #55: One-On-One Scramble

Objective: To improve defensive skills and conditioning levels.

Description: The coach should divide the team into two groups. The two groups form a line under separate baskets. The first person in each line should begin at half-court, one on offense and one on defense. All action takes place at full speed. The offensive player works toward his basket and tries to score. If he succeeds, the defender goes to the end of the line under that basket. If the defender forces a turnover or gets a rebound, he goes on offense to the other end of the court against his opponent. If either player scores, the first player in the line under that basket grabs the ball and "inbounds" it by tossing it off the backboard. He and the shooter then compete for the rebound. If the shooter gets the rebound, he goes on offense at the same basket. If the inbounder gets the rebound, he attacks at the opposite end of the court. The drill may be run for a set period of time, or until one of the players scores a prescribed number of points. The coach may also split the team into four groups and run the drill on two side-by-side courts.

Coaching Point:

- This drill is an excellent drill to be used for practicing defensive skills and improving conditioning levels early in the season.

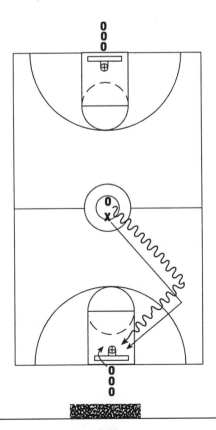

Drill #56: Cut Off the Drive

Objective: To improve a defender's ability to force a dribbler to alter his line of attack.

Description: The coach should split the team into two groups, each working at one end of the court. Half the group should form a line at one of the offensive wing positions. The other players in the group, who will begin the drill on defense, should form a line behind the baseline. The first defender should assume a good defensive stance in front of the first offensive player. The offensive player is allowed only one move, a strong drive to the hoop. He may go to either side of the defender, but must try to keep a straight course. The defender tries to herd the dribbler to either the baseline or the middle of the court using quick footwork and good, aggressive body positioning. Play continues until there is a score or change of possession. The players then go to the end of the opposite line.

Coaching Points:

- The emphasis should be on quick footwork and good defensive body position.
- The coach should encourage aggressive play, but blow the whistle on obvious fouls.

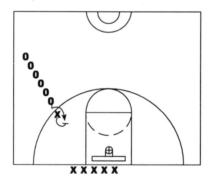

Drill #57: Denying the Pass

Objective: To teach defenders to disrupt the offense by denying the pass.

Description: The primary players in this drill are one offensive and one defensive player. A point guard (PG) is added whose sole function in the drill is to pass the ball. The players are positioned as shown in the diagram below. The defender overplays the offensive player to deny the pass. The offensive player may attempt to get open by making cuts or going back door. The defender should be in position to deny the pass no matter where the offensive player goes.

Coaching Point:

- The emphasis should be on making sure the defender is always in position to see the ball and deny the pass.

CHAPTER 7

REBOUNDING DRILLS

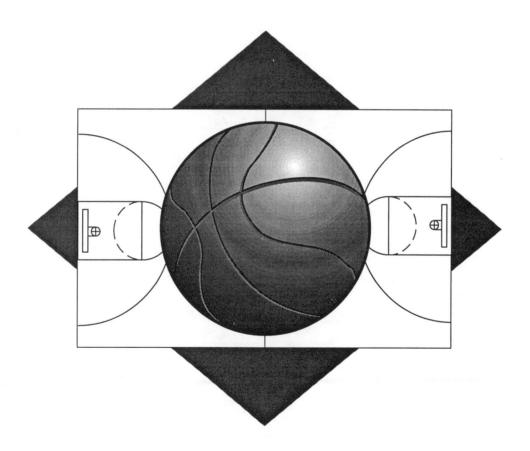

Drill #58: Rebound and Get It Out

Objective: To develop a rebounder's ability to secure the ball, turn in the air, and make an accurate outlet pass.

Description: The team should be split into pairs made up of one guard (G) and one pivot player (C). The whole group may take turns at one end of the court, or the team may utilize both baskets. C is positioned approximately five feet from the basket, and G is stationed at the top of the key. A coach or manager tosses up a missed shot. C goes up for the rebound and G breaks to the appropriate sideline to receive an outlet pass. C secures the rebound at the highest point possible and turns his body in the air so he lands in a position to quickly make the outlet pass. The shooter should vary the location of the shot so the players will have to determine which sideline the outlet pass should go to.

Coaching Point:

- The guards should take care to go the proper sideline so the ball is never passed across the basket.

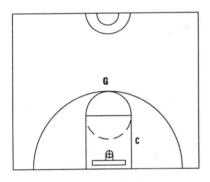

Diagram A

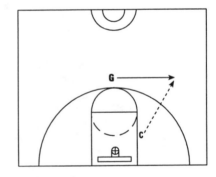

Diagram B

Drill #59: Controlling the Tip

Objective: To improve a rebounder's ability to tip the ball and keep it under control.

Description: The team should be divided into groups of four, each positioned at a basket. Each group forms a single line beginning in the midpost area. The first player in line acts as a shooter. He tosses the ball off the backboard, and the next player in line moves forward and tips the ball off the backboard. He keeps jumping and tipping, keeping the ball in play as long as possible. Each player takes a turn as the shooter, and the drill continues for a predetermined amount of time. The coach may instruct players to alternate hands with every tip or change the hand used with every rotation.

Coaching Point:

• The emphasis should be placed on keeping the action as high on the backboard as possible. Players should jump as high as they can.

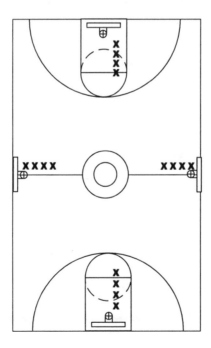

Drill #60: Numbers Game

Objective: To improve a defensive rebounder's awareness of both his opponent and the ball.

Description: The team should be divided into groups of five, each working at its own basket. Two players are on offense, two on defense, with the fifth player stationed at the free-throw line. The other players are in the mid post area. The offensive players are given ten seconds to get open. If they break free under the basket, the player at the free-throw line may pass to them. If they score, each offensive player gets a point. If no pass is made within ten seconds, the player at the line throws up a missed shot. As soon as the shot goes up, the offensive players each raise a hand with one or more fingers held up. They then go for the rebound and earn a point if they are successful. Defenders should remain aware of the location of their opponent. They attempt to block out and get the rebound. They earn a point if they secure the rebound, and a bonus point if both defenders correctly call out the number of fingers their opponent held up. Players rotate through the positions until they have played each role three times. The points are then totaled to determine the winner. The drill may also be run with a coach at the free-throw line and the team split into groups of four.

Coaching Point:

- The coach should rotate between the groups and emphasize correct rebounding position.

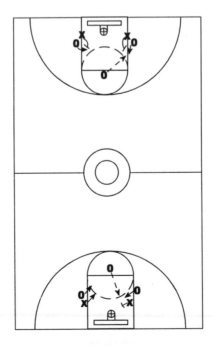

Drill #61: Simulated Line Drill

Objective: To teach the fundamentals of sound rebounding techniques.

Description: The team should be divided into groups of four. The groups form evenly spaced lines behind the baseline. The first player in each line assumes a good defensive position and, on the coach's command, sprints about ten feet onto the court and assumes a good rebounding position. The coach is holding a ball, and with it he indicates which side of the court the ball is on. When he raises the ball above his head, it signifies that a shot has been taken. Players simulate a good block out, jump to bring down the rebound, and protect the ball. They simulate an outlet pass and resume a good defensive position. The second player in each line moves to the baseline, and repeats the drill with the first group. The drill continues until the last group reaches the far baseline.

Coaching Point:

- The coach should take the time to make any necessary corrections in technique.

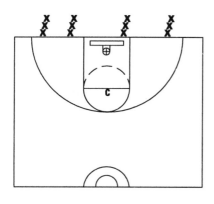

Diagram A

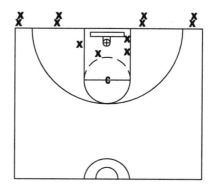

Diagram B

Drill #62: Individual Tip Drill

Objective: To improve a rebounder's ability to tip the ball and keep it under control.

Description: The coach should divide the team into groups to be stationed at every available basket. Working individually, each player tosses the ball against the backboard and attempts to keep it in play. Players should keep the action as high on the backboard as possible by jumping as high as they can. The player's arm should be fully extended when tipping the ball, and he should alternate between his left and right hands. As skill levels progress, the players may be required to tip the ball from one side of the backboard to the other, sliding back and forth under the basket between tips. This drill may also be used as a conditioning drill.

Coaching Point:

- When using this drill for conditioning early in the season, the coach may choose to group two or three players at a basket to allow players time to rest.

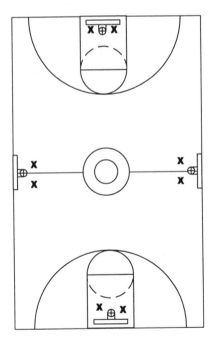

Drill #63: Jump and Jump Some More

Objective: To improve conditioning levels and leg strength.

Description: The players should be divided into pairs, which are distributed among all available baskets. One player has the ball, and the other acts as the rebounder. The offensive player puts up ten jump-shots, and the rebounder assumes a good block-out position on each shot. If a rebound is made, the ball is returned to the shooter as if executing an outlet pass. If the shot is made, the rebounder grabs the ball, steps over the baseline, and inbounds the ball to the shooter as quickly as possible. The shooter should move between shots to force the rebounder to locate him quickly. As soon as the ten shots are taken, the two players each execute ten in-place high jumps and then switch positions. Some coaches choose to have two or three players shoot at a time and retrieve their own shots.

Coaching Point:

- The coach may give a jump and reach test at the beginning of the season and repeat the test at intervals to measure progress in jumping ability.

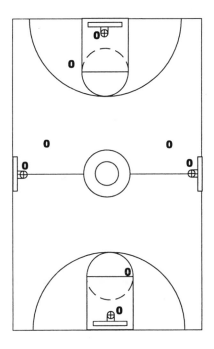

Drill #64: Controlled Three-on-Three

Objective: To improve a rebounder's techniques in blocking out and protecting the ball after a rebound.

Description: This drill is designed primarily for forwards and centers. The coach should form groups made up of one center and two forwards. One group begins the drill on offense, another on defense. A coach or manager has the ball anywhere on the perimeter, and attempts a shot. The offensive players try to cut by their defenders for the rebound. The defenders, whose eyes should be on both the ball and their opponent, turn one shoulder perpendicular to the offensive player, then pivot in the direction of their opponent's penetration and assume a good block out position. If a defender gets the rebound, he should bring it down with his elbows extended and the ball in the protected position under his chin. The groups then reverse roles and the drill continues. The drill may also be run in a three-on-three game, with the players working on getting a good shot as well as rebounding techniques.

Coaching Point:

- Since this drill emphasizes fundamentals, the coach should stop the action to correct any errors in technique.

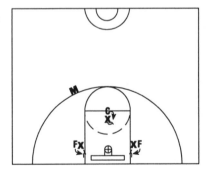

Drill #65: Short Clock Two-on-Two

Objective: To improve a rebounder's techniques in blocking out and protecting the ball after a rebound.

Description: This drill is designed for perimeter players. The coach should divide the perimeter players into pairs—a point guard (G) who is positioned near the top of the key and a forward (F) who is located in the high wing area. Two other players assume a good defensive position on G and F. The coach or manager has a stopwatch and tosses the ball to either offensive player. The offense has ten seconds to put up a shot. The use of the short clock focuses the drill more on rebounding. After the shot goes up, the offensive players cut to the boards. The defenders pivot in the direction of their opponent's penetration and assume a good block-out position. If a defender gets the rebound, he should bring it down with his elbows extended outward and the ball in the protected position under his chin. On the second rotation of the drill, the players reverse offensive and defensive roles.

Coaching Point:

- The drill should emphasize to defenders the importance of simultaneously seeing both the ball and their opponent when the shot is taken.

Drill #66: Rebound, Pass, and Run

Objective: To develop a rebounder's ability to secure the ball, turn in the air, and make an accurate outlet pass.

Description: The coach should divide the team into groups of four, each made up of two guards (G) and two post players (F). The post players are positioned on either side of the lane in the mid post area, while the guards are stationed side by side at the top of the key. A coach or manager tosses an errant shot to either side of the backboard. The F on that side of the lane goes up for the rebound, and the appropriate guard breaks to the sideline for the outlet pass. F secures the rebound at the highest point possible, turns his body in the air, and makes a quick outlet pass upon landing. The other guard breaks to the middle to receive the second pass, as if starting the fast break.

Coaching Point:

- The guards should go to the proper sideline so the ball is never passed across the basket.

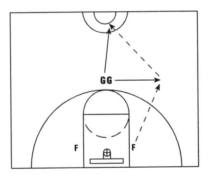

Drill #67: Saving the Ball

Objective: To teach the proper method of saving the ball from going out of bounds on the defensive end of the floor.

Description: The players should be divided into two groups and form two lines facing the baseline. The coach bounces the ball toward the baseline. The first player in the first line attempts to save the ball. The first player in the second line comes to the ball as a receiver, calling out to help his teammate locate him. The player from the first line saves the ball only if there is no opponent in the way and if he makes eye contact with his teammate. The coach may act as a mock opponent to add difficulty to the drill. The drill may also be run with the players facing the sideline.

Coaching Point:

• Since this drill is being run on the defensive end of the floor, players should never save the ball without making eye contact with the receiver.

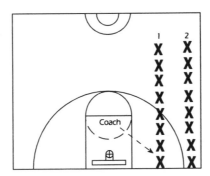

CHAPTER 8

POST DEFENSE DRILLS

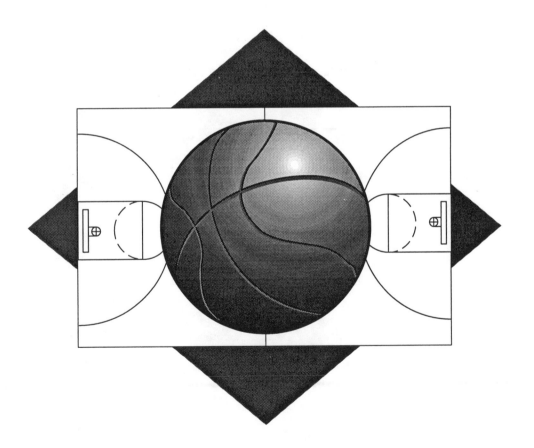

Drill #68: Double Trouble

Objective: To practice double-teaming the post; to teach the proper rotation of defenders after the double-team occurs.

Description: This five-on-five drill begins with the players positioned as shown in the diagram below and the ball in the point guard's (PG) hands. The defense allows PG to pass into the center (C) on the low post. The primary responsibility of PG's defender is to deny the return pass. The shooting guard's (SG) defender drops down from the top of the lane and sets up the double-team with C's defender. They should not allow C to split the double-team. The power forward's (PF) defender plays the passing lane between PF and C, leaving C only the desperation pass to SG or the small forward (SF). On a pass from C to the perimeter, SF's defender is prepared to rotate to cover either SG or SF. SG's defender leaves the double-team and covers the opponent left open.

Coaching Point:

- The coach may choose to have SG's defender create the double-team as soon as the pass is made or when C begins his dribble.

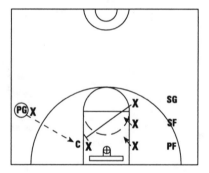

Drill #69: Defending the Baseline Attack

Objective: To improve a post defender's techniques in footwork and denying the ball to an opponent.

Description: This drill involves two post defenders, two offensive post players, and two offensive wing players, positioned as shown in the diagram below. The ball is in the hands of either wing. He looks to pass to an open post player, and the defenders work to stay in position to deny their opponents the ball from the baseline side. The offside post defender should be able to see both his man and the ball and be prepared to help at any time. The wing players may drive at any time or pass cross court to the other wing, forcing the defenders to adjust. After a basket or a change of possession, the ball goes to the opposite wing to repeat the drill.

Coaching Point:

- The coach should make sure the post defenders are adjusting properly to the ball and maintaining a good defensive position.

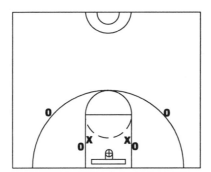

Drill #70: Forcing the Outside Shot

Objective: To teach perimeter defenders to help defend the post by playing back and forth between their opponent and the post player.

Description: The squad should be split into two teams, positioned as shown in Diagram A. In the drill, the point guard (PG) is not considered a good outside shooter. PG's defender allows a pass into the center (C) and quickly moves to double-team the post. If the pass goes back out to PG, his defender hustles back to interfere with the next pass. Double-teaming C ensures he will not get an easy shot and forces PG to beat the defense from the outside. All other defenders are prepared to deny a pass or help on cutters through the lane. C's defender should play physical defense, forcing C as far from the basket as possible. If PG cuts through the post as shown in Diagram B, his defender stays with him until he is midway through the lane, then releases to double-team C. All other defenders rotate accordingly.

Coaching Point:

- The offside defenders should sag into the lane and be prepared to help if needed.

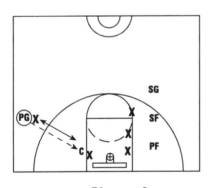

Diagram A

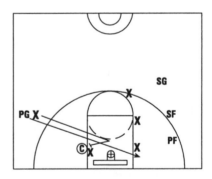

Diagram B

Drill #71: Post Movement

Objective: To teach post defenders the proper footwork to deny passes from the perimeter.

Description: This drill pits one post defender against an offensive post player and three perimeter offensive players, positioned as shown in the diagram below. The drill should initially be run at half-speed. The point guard (PG) has the ball and passes to either wing player. The defender must quickly get into position to deny the pass into the post. He should chest his opponent and force him away from the basket, keeping him from getting free on the baseline for the pass. As the footwork becomes more familiar to the post defender, PG and the wings may pass cross court and increase the tempo of the drill to full speed to increase the level of difficulty.

Coaching Point:

- This drill should be stopped to correct any errors in the footwork or body position of the defender.

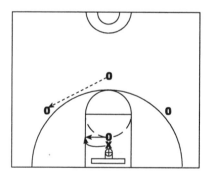

Drill #72: High Post "D"

Objective: To improve a post defender's techniques against a high post offense.

Description: This drill pits a high post player and two guards against a similar defense, and should initially be run at half-speed. The guards pass the ball between each other, while the post player slides back and forth looking for a pass from the perimeter. The post defender should adjust to the ball and his opponent to deny the pass. The offensive guards are not permitted to shoot, drive or cut to the basket, or screen for each other. The defensive guards sag back and play loose defense on the ball. The post defender should not give any ground to his opponent but should keep him in the high post area. Only if a pass gets into the high post should the defender step back to guard against the drive. If the post player drives instead of taking the shot, the defender should try to force him away from where he wants to go.

Coaching Point:

- The coach should make any corrections in techniuqe as necessary.

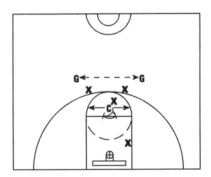

Drill #73: High-Low-Anywhere Five-On-Five

Objective: To improve a post player's ability to react and maintain a correct defensive position.

Description: This drill should initially be run at half-speed, and involves five offensive and five defensive players positioned as shown in the diagram below. The ball begins with one of the guards and is passed around the perimeter, with all the offensive perimeter players looking for a chance to get the ball into the post. The perimeter offensive players are not allowed to shoot, drive or cut to the basket, or screen for each other. The offensive post player may move anywhere in the lane, restricted only by the three-second rule. The post defender should move quickly to deny the pass and maintain proper body position on the opponent and the ball. He should try to alter the desired route of the offensive post player. After a few minutes at half-speed, this drill should be run at full speed with an emphasis on rapid ball movement.

Coaching Point:

- While the drill is run at half-speed, the coach should stop the action to make corrections. The full-speed drill should be run uninterrupted, with corrections made at the conclusion of the drill.

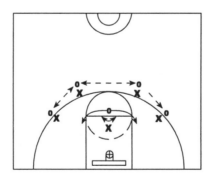

Drill #74: Post Double-Team From the Baseline

Objective: To practice double-teaming the post; to teach the proper rotation of the defenders after the double-team occurs.

Description: Two five-player teams should position themselves as shown in Diagram A. The point guard (PG) has the ball, and is allowed to pass to the center (C) at the low post. C's defender is guarding him from behind and denying the pass to the center of the lane, forcing the pass to go to the baseline side. After the pass is completed, the power forward's (PF) defender sets up a double-team with C's defender. They should not allow C to split the double-team for an easy basket. PG's defender denies the return pass to PG, and the other two defenders rotate down the lane. The small forward's (SF) defender plays the passing lane between C and PF, leaving only SF and the shooting guard (SG) open for a pass out of the double-team. SG's defender is ready to recover to his man, while the other two helping defenders are ready to rotate back to their original positions as well (Diagram B).

Coaching Point:

* The coach may choose to have PF's defender break to double-team on the pass or when C has begun his dribble.
* Whenever the ball gets into the low post, all defenders should sag into the lane to be ready to help.

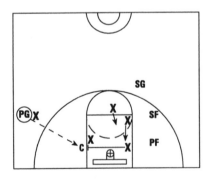

Diagram A

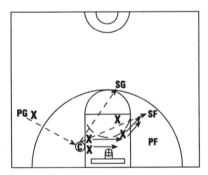

Diagram B

Drill #75: Helping In the Post

Objective: To teach defenders to help in post defense on an offside break through the lane.

Description: This drill involves a guard (G), an offside low post player (F), and a lone defender, positioned as shown in Diagram A. The guard begins the drill with the ball. F fakes to the basket and cuts through the lane to the opposite side for a pass from G. The defender must rotate into the proper position to deny the pass. When denied the pass, F breaks down through the lane as shown in Diagram B. The defender must pivot correctly and slide down the lane with F to continue to deny the pass. After the second denial, F slides back to his original position, while the defender adjusts back to his help position. Three new players rotate in, and the drill is continued. The drill should be run on both sides of the court.

Coaching Point:

- The emphasis should be placed on proper footwork by the defender.

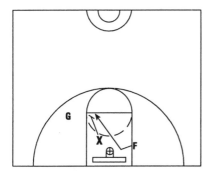

Diagram A

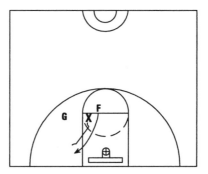

Diagram B

Drill #76: Two-On-Two Within Five-On-Five

Objective: To teach both individual and team defense against a two-man inside-outside game.

Description: Two five-player teams should be positioned as shown in the diagram below. The point guard (PG) has the ball and attempts to run a two-player game with the center (C). The shooting guard (SG), small forward (SF), and power forward (PF) have cleared to the weakside and are looking to cut or screen and cut to the lane. PG's defender attempts to make the pass to C as difficult as possible. C's defender fronts the post, trying to deny the pass, hold his position, and force C to the baseline. The weakside defenders are in a help position and should be prepared to help in the post against cutters and lobs. If a lob pass does get to C, PF's defender should be in place to execute a double-team when the pass arrives.

Coaching Point:

- The coach may choose to forbid perimeter shots to emphasize action in the post.

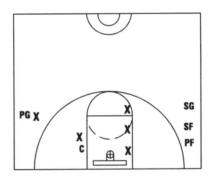

Drill #77: Three-On-Three Within Five-On-Five

Objective: To teach both individual and team defense against a three-man triangle game.

Description: Two five-player teams should be positioned as shown in the diagram below with the ball in the point guard's (PG) hands. PG's first option is to get the ball into the center (C) at the low post. His second option is to pass to the shooting guard (SG) in the corner. PG's defender makes it as difficult as possible to make the pass into C. SG's defender overplays SG to disrupt the passing lane and deny the pass to the corner. C's defender fronts the post, trying to deny the pass, hold position, and force C to the baseline. The men guarding the small forward (SF) and power forward (PF) are in a help position to assist against cutters and lobs. If a lob pass does get into the post, PF's defender should be in place to execute a double-team when the pass arrives.

Coaching Point:

- The coach should be sure the weakside defenders rotate correctly to help on cutters and lobs.
- If the ball gets into the deep post, all defenders should sag to the lane to help.

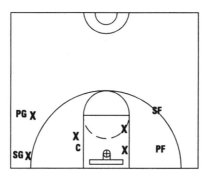

Drill #78: Inside Help and Recover

Objective: To teach the techniques used by a perimeter defender to help inside on the post and recover to his man.

Description: This drill involves an offensive wing player and a post player and their defensive counterparts. The offense is restricted to one side of the court. The post defender plays behind his man toward the ballside and attempts to deny the pass into the post. The offensive post must work to get open for a pass from his teammate. If the pass gets into the post, the perimeter defender collapses inside to double-team the post. If the ball is passed back out, the perimeter defender must recover quickly to his own man.

Coaching Point:

- When the ball gets into the post, the perimeter defender should keep his back to the baseline in order to see the whole court.

CHAPTER 9

DEFENDING AGAINST THE SCREEN

Drill #79: Slide-Through Drill

Objective: To teach perimeter defenders how to cope with back screens using the slide-through technique.

Description: In this drill, two offensive guards pass the ball between each other, and two defenders pressure and sag accordingly. On the coach's command, one guard passes the ball to his counterpart and cuts behind for a handoff. The player defending the screener takes one step back, allowing his teammate to slide through the screen and remain with his man. The first defender quickly steps back up to guard the screener, who still has the ball. The ballhandler dribbles across to balance the floor, and the drill is run in the other direction. After several repetitions, the guard receiving the handoff can move off the screen in any direction he desires, forcing his opponent to react accordingly. The screener may also be allowed to fake the handoff and keep the ball. Two-on-two play is continued until a score is made.

Coaching Point:

- The coach should be sure the defenders understand the timing of the slide-through maneuver before allowing freedom of movement by the offense.

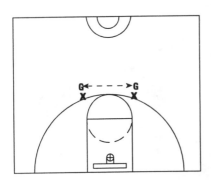

Diagram A

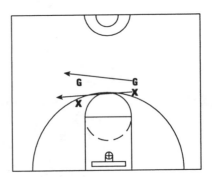

Diagram B

Drill #80: Man-to-Man Double-Screen "D"

Objective: To teach and practice two methods of defending against a double-down screen maneuver.

Description: Two five-player teams should be positioned as shown in Diagram A. The power forward (PF) and the center (C) set a double screen on their defenders so the small forward (SF) can scrape his defender off as he cuts to the free-throw line looking for a pass from the point guard (PG). The defense avoids switching because of the size advantage it would give the offense in the lane. PG's defender attempts to force the ball to the sideline, while the shooting guard's (SG) defender denies the pass to SG. The players guarding PF and C play on the ballside shoulder of their men. The small forward's (SF) defender tries to go around the screen, keeping his body between SF and the ball. In Diagram B, SF's defender splits the double screen in an attempt to deny the pass. The responsibilities of the other defenders remain the same, except that C's defender plays head-to-head defense in an attempt to force C out to make room for his teammate to split the screen.

Coaching Point:

• The physical play necessary on the part of PF and C's defenders to handle the screeners should be emphasized.

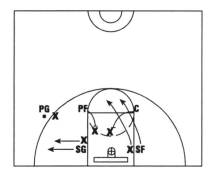

Diagram A

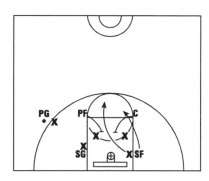

Diagram B

Drill #81: Upscreen "D"

Objective: To teach and practice two methods of defending a backscreen set for the high post.

Description: This three-on-three drill involves a point guard (G), a wing (F), and an offensive high post player (C) and their defenders, positioned as shown in Diagram A. The wing comes from the baseline to set a screen for C at the high post. Using his ballside shoulder, F's defender forces F away from his desired area. C's defender hears the screen is coming and plays C's ballside shoulder. The post defender maintains position and keeps C from cutting straight to the lane. G's defender forces G to the sideline. In Diagram B, F's defender forces F toward the ball. C's defender goes to the weakside off the screen and keeps his body in position to deny C the pass in the lane.

Coaching Points:

- The defenders should try to avoid switching in order to keep size match-ups in favor of the defense.
- Good communication is more helpful against the backscreen than any other action.

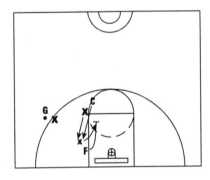

Diagram A

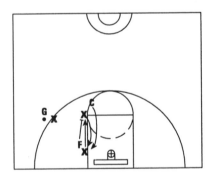

Diagram B

Drill #82: Screen and Talk "D"

Objective: To practice various techniques used in defending the screen away from the ball; to provide the opportunity for players to practice their defensive signals.

Description: This drill involves a point guard (PG) and two offensive wings (F) and their defenders. The point guard passes to either wing, and the ball continues around the perimeter quickly, forcing the defenders to react accordingly. On the coach's command, the point guard passes to one wing and moves down to set a screen for the other wing away from the ball. The defenders must communicate how they are going to deal with the screen. The defender may fight over the top of the screen, slide through, or go around it. The defenders should also practice switching on the screen, concentrating on keeping themselves in position to see both their man and the ball. As the drill continues, the offense may choose to screen on or away from the ball and up or down.

Coaching Point:

- Early in the season, this is a good teaching drill. As the season progresses, it is useful for reinforcing the verbal signals and strategies the team uses to deal with screens.

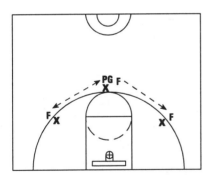

Diagram A

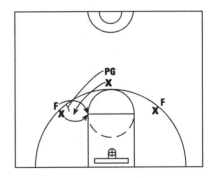

Diagram B

Drill #83: Cut Off the Screen

Objective: To teach and practice defending the pick and roll by getting to the screen faster than the ballhandler.

Description: This drill begins with two five-player teams positioned as shown in the diagram below. As the center (C) starts to move to set the screen, his defender communicates to the point guard's (PG) defender that the screener is on his way. PG's defender then quickly gets between the screener and the ballhandler to cut off the screen. C's defender then circles down to cut off the sideline drive and, if possible, creates a double-team on PG, leaving C free. If C moves out high to give PG a passing option, the defenders rotate. The shooting guard's (SG) defender moves cross court to pick up C, while the other weakside defenders shift up the lane to guard against cutters. If C breaks low down the lane, the power forward's (PF) defender comes across to cut him off, while SG and SF's defender shift down the lane to guard against cutters.

Coaching Point:

- The emphasis should be place on executing a solid double-team, rotating quickly, and communicating.

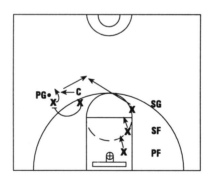

Drill #84: Beat the Screener to the Ball

Objective: To teach and practice defending the pick and roll by executing a quick double-team maneuver on the ball.

Description: This five-on-five drill begins with the players positioned as shown in Diagram A. As the center (C) starts to move over to set the screen, his defender sprints to beat him to the ball. The point guard's (PG) defender forces PG toward the screen, and the defenders aggressively double-team PG. C's defender should stay on the high side of PG when setting the double-team. C will either move to the lane or shift out high. If he rolls low, the power forward's (PF) defender crosses over from the offside to cover, and the other two weakside defenders shift down the lane looking for cutters. Diagram B shows the rotation that occurs if C shifts high. The shooting guard's (SG) defender runs from the offside to cover, and SF and PF's defenders shift up the lane to guard against cutters.

Coaching Points:

- The coach should emphasize setting a solid double-team.
- The emphasis should also be placed on the quick execution of the double-team maneuver on the ball.

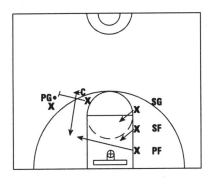

Diagram A

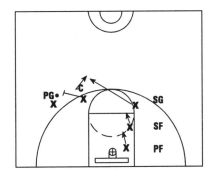

Diagram B

Drill #85: Force the Screen High

Objective: To teach and practice defending the pick and roll by avoiding the switch and going around the screen.

Description: This drill involves four players—two on offense, an offensive point guard (PG) and center (C), and two on defense, positioned as shown in the diagram below. As C moves over to set the screen, his defender anticipates the maneuver and forces him to set the pick higher than he would like. This action forces PG to go higher around the screen than normal and allows the defensive guard time to go around the pick and stay with his man. PG's defender tries to move around the screen quickly enough to get into position to keep the ball on the same side of the court. C's defender stays in position to deny C the roll down the lane and forces any roll maneuver to the sideline.

Coaching Points:

- The coach should emphasize that tough, physical defense is necessary to force the screen high.
- Communication between defenders is essential.

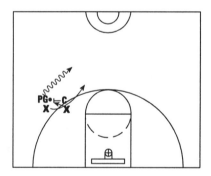

Drill #86: Pop-Out and Double

Objective: To teach and practice the techniques involved in executing a double-team off a pop-out switch.

Description: This five-on-five drill begins with the players positioned as shown in Diagram A. The point guard (PG) is dribbling the ball. The center (C) moves over to set a screen, and is followed closely by his defender, who bumps him as aggressively as possible and pops out on PG, trying to keep the ball on the same side of the court. PG's defender follows the ball and helps double-team PG. The power forward's (PF) defender should rotate across the lane to pick up C as he rolls off the screen. The other weakside defenders rotate down into the lane looking for cutters. If PG is forced out high (Diagram B), C's defender must decide how long to stay with the double-team before retreating to the paint. If PG successfully gets rid of the ball, C's defender must immediately rotate back to the lane, and all other defenders hustle to their men.

Coaching Points:

- The coach should emphasize the importance of the timing and aggressiveness on the pop-out move.
- Good communication between the defenders should also be stressed.

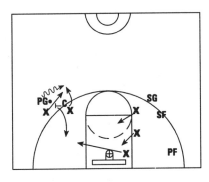

Diagram A

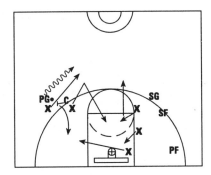

Diagram B

Drill #87: Over the Top and Help

Objective: To improve the players' abilities to defend a screen on the ball.

Description: This drill involves four players—an offensive point guard and a wing and their two defenders. No switching is allowed. The wing sets a screen for the ball, and his defender follows closely. As the screen is set, the screener's defender cheats off his man and slightly into the point guard's path in an attempt to delay the dribble. This action should give the point guard's defender time to fight over the top of the screen and regain proper position on his man. This drill may be run simultaneously at both ends of the court. The drill should also be reversed and started with the ball in the wing's hands.

Coaching Point:

* The coach should stress the importance of good communication between the defenders.

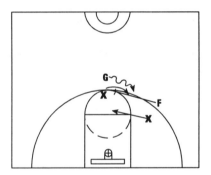

Drill #88: Wing Back Screen Drill

Objective: To teach perimeter defenders to deal with back screens using the slide-through technique.

Description: This drill involves a point guard (PG) and two wing players (F) and their defenders. PG dribbles from side to side near the top of the key and passes back and forth to both wings. The wings may also pass cross court if the pass is open. Early in the drill, no shots are allowed. The defenders pressure and sag accordingly. On the coach's command, PG passes to either wing and breaks behind him for a handoff. F's defender takes a step backward, allowing his teammate to slide through the screen, then steps up to pressure F, who still has the ball. F moves out to the point position and passes back to PG to run the screen in the other direction. The drill then shifts to the other side of the floor. After several repetitions, the player receiving the handoff can move off the screen in any direction he desires, forcing the defenders to react accordingly. The drill may also be run allowing the screener to fake the handoff and the offside wing the opportunity to move without the ball to get open for a pass.

Coaching Point:

- The coach should be sure the players understand the timing of the slide-through technique before allowing the offensive players freedom of movement.

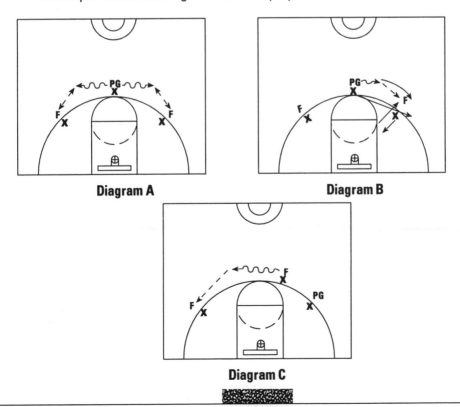

Diagram A   Diagram B

Diagram C

Drill #89: Post Downscreen Drill

Objective: To improve the defenders' abilities to deal with a downscreen from the perimeter to the post using a variation of the slide-through technique.

Description: This drill involves four players—an offensive wing and a low post player and their two defenders. A point guard is at the ballside top of the key to pass the ball. No switching is allowed. The wing breaks down to set a screen for his teammate. The wing defender moves with his man at an angle that allows the post defender to slide through the screen and remain with his man. The defensive wing remains between his man and the ball to deny the pass into the lane. The point guard attempts to pass to either player if one is open. If neither is open, the players rotate back to their original positions, and the drill begins again. After a few repetitions, the offensive players can break and roll off the screens in any direction they desire to get open for the pass. This drill may be run simultaneously at both ends of the court.

Coaching Point:

- The coach should stress the importance of good communication between the defenders.

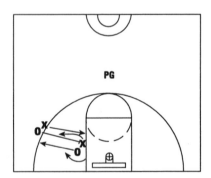

Drill #90: Defending Split-Post Maneuvers

Objective: To teach and practice two methods of defending against split-post maneuvers when the ball is in the high post.

Description: This three-on-three drill involves a point guard (PG), a wing player (F), and a high post player (C) and their three defenders, positioned as shown in Diagram A. The best defense against a split-post maneuver is to deny the ball to C at the high post. C's defender does his best to deny the pass and force C out as high as possible. The defender should be very physical with C. Once C gets the ball, his defender plays a step off him, ready to help out as needed. The other defenders keep their bodies between their opponents and the ball at all times. When PG and F cross, their defenders switch, being careful to maintain inside position on their new men. Diagram B illustrates a more physical approach and increases the chances of being called for a foul. The post defender's assignment remains the same. The other defenders play their own men even more physically and deny them a path to their desired spot on the floor. They do not switch, but stay with their own men.

Coaching Point:

- The defenders should bump the cutters to disrupt the timing of the play as much as possible.

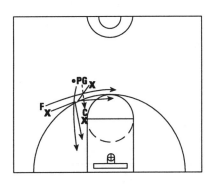

Diagram A

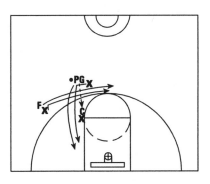

Diagram B

CHAPTER 10

SWITCHING DRILLS

Drill #91: Switching Double-Screen "D"

Objective: To teach and practice two methods of defending against a double-down screen maneuver.

Description: This drill involves five-on-five competition with the players positioned as shown in Diagram A. The point guard's (PG) defender plays aggressive pressure defense, attempting to force the ball to the sideline. The shooting guard's (SG) defender stays between his man and the ball to deny the pass. The high post defenders play the ballside shoulder of their respective men. As the small forward (SF) comes around the screen, the power forward's (PF) defender switches out to deny the pass to SF. The center's (C) defender shifts over to PF and positions his body to deny the pass. SF's defender then shifts to C's ballside shoulder. Another option is shown in Diagram B. PF's defender is alert to cut off SF if he cuts under, rather than around, the screen. If SF goes around, SG's defender leaves his man and beats SF to his desired spot on the floor. SF's defender moves out to cover SG.

Coaching Point:

- The players should switch back to their original man as soon as possible to avoid bad size match-ups.

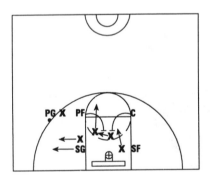

Diagram A

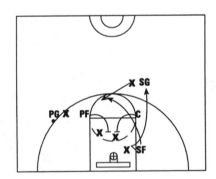

Diagram B

Drill #92: Switch, No-Switch Offside Screen

Objective: To teach and practice defending against the offside V-cut and backscreen maneuver.

Description: This drill involves six players—a point guard (PG), a wing (F), and an offensive post player (C) and their defenders. When C moves out to set a backscreen on the defensive wing, the post defender lets his teammate know the screen is coming. F uses a V-cut maneuver to try to make his defender fall for the fake. F's defender stays with his man long enough to be certain he is forced to go high around the screen. The post defender follows C to the screen, and pops out on F as he cuts high off the screen. The defender forces F to go as high as possible to look for a pass from PG. After the switch, F's defender stays with C. If the players decide not to switch, the post defender forces C high in an attempt to destroy C's angle to the screen. F's defender makes certain F cuts low around the screen and stays with his own man. In a five-on-five situation, the wing defender would get help from the ballside post if he were beaten.

Coaching Points:

- Good communication is extremely important against the backscreen.
- The players should switch back to their own men as soon as possible to keep size match-ups in their favor.

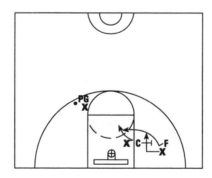

Drill #93: Perimeter Rotation

Objective: To teach perimeter defenders the proper rotation necessary to shift from a deny position to a help position.

Description: This drill involves six players—a point guard and two wings on offense and their defensive counterparts. Both wing defenders begin the drill in a deny position. The guard's defender participates only to add reality to the drill and should not attempt to disrupt his opponent's ball movement. The guard dribbles toward the wing, and the wing defender aggressively plays the passing lane to deny the ball to his opponent. The other defensive wing slides into the lane in the help position. He is still in position to deny a pass to his man, and can see both his man and the ball. He is also in position to help on the drive or cut into the lane. The offensive guard works the ball to both sides of the court during the drill. As players become familiar with the rotations, The defensive guard may be allowed to play aggressive defense, turning the drill into a full scrimmage.

Coaching Point:

* The coach should emphasize the proper shift from a deny position to a help position and pay particular attention to body positioning.

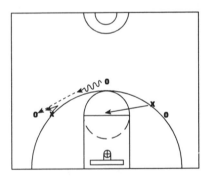

Drill #94: Switch, No-Switch Backscreen "D"

Objective: To teach and practice defending against a backscreen.

Description: This drill involves six players—an offensive point guard (PG), a wing (F), and a post player (C) and their defenders, positioned as shown in Diagram A. When C moves up to set a backscreen on the wing defender, C's defender warns his teammate and attempts to force C lower than he would like. As F cuts off the screen looking for the pass, C's defender pops out and switches, trying to head off penetration to the lane. If he is unsuccessful, he stays with F, positioning himself between F and the ball. The wing defender rotates back, staying between the ball and C if C rolls to the lane. PG's defender has been attempting to force PG to the sideline while staying in position to deny a pass to the lane. Diagram B illustrates the action if the defenders do not switch. The defensive guard's task remains the same. The post defender physically bumps C, staying with him as long as possible. As F cuts off the screen, C's defender jumps out to help until F's defender can recover. F's defender must fight either over or under the screen to get back to his man. C's defender should recover to his man, staying between C and the ball.

Coaching Points:

- Backscreens are difficult to defend, and communication between the defenders is critical.
- Players should switch back to their original men as soon as possible to keep size match-ups in the defense's favor.

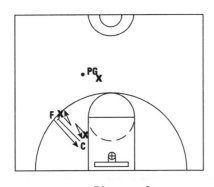

Diagram A

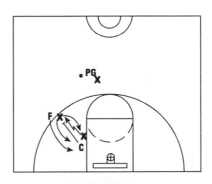

Diagram B

Drill #95: Help!!!

Objective: To teach and practice defenders' help responsibilities against the drive.

Description: This drill involves eight players—four offensive perimeter players (two wings and two guards), and their four defenders. The offensive players should be spaced around the free-throw lane. The right guard has the ball and attempts to drive to the basket. The defenders sag and rotate as needed. The ballhandler's defender, if beaten on the drive, must yell "Help" to be certain his teammates are aware of the problem. After a made shot or change of possession, the ball comes back out to be passed around the perimeter again. Any offensive player may drive to the basket, forcing different defensive rotations.

Coaching Point:

• The coach should be certain all the offensive players drive to the basket at some point so more defensive rotations can be practiced.

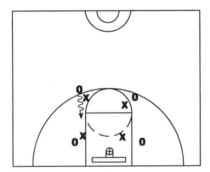

Drill #96: Force and Rotate

Objective: To teach and practice defending the pick and roll by forcing the screen high and using a cross court switch and rotation.

Description: This five-on-five drill begins with the players positioned as shown in the diagram below. As the center (C) moves over to set a screen for the point guard (PG), C's defender anticipates the maneuver and forces C to set the pick higher than he would like. This action forces PG to go higher around the screen than normal and allows the shooting guard's (SG) defender time to come from the weakside and switch onto PG, forcing him to keep the ball on the same side of the court. As PG commits to using the screen, PG's defender rotates back into the lane to help against possible cutters. C's defender stays in position to keep C from rolling to the lane. The small forward's (SF) defender rotates up the lane looking to intercept a pass to SG or SF, and the power forward's (PF) defender stays low looking for cutters, ready to help in the lane.

Coaching Points:

- The coach should emphasize the aggressive, physical defense that must be played by C's defender to force the screen high, and the speed of the cross court switch by SG's defender.
- The defenders should communicate during the switch.

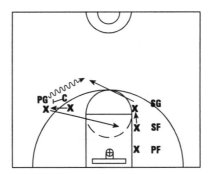

Drill #97: Switch, Double, and Rotate

Objective: To teach and practice defending the pick and roll using a switch in conjunction with a double-team.

Description: This five-on-five drill begins with the players positioned as shown in the diagram below. The center (C) moves over to set a screen, and his defender moves quickly with him. C's defender bumps C as hard as he can get away with and executes a slide switch maneuver to stop the point guard's (PG) penetration down the lane. PG's defender moves quickly to the ballside of C to prevent the pass and roll to the basket. The shooting guard's (SG) defender leaves his man and runs over to set a double-team on PG with C's defender. The other weakside defenders rotate slightly up the lane. The small forward's (SF) defender is looking to intercept a desperation pass from the double-teamed PG and should be alert for cutters. The power forward's (PF) defender should also be on guard for cutters. If PG successfully gets rid of the ball, C's defender rotates back to the paint and all defenders recover to their men as quickly as possible.

Coaching Point:

- The coach should emphasize the timing of the double-team and stress the importance of good communication among the defenders.

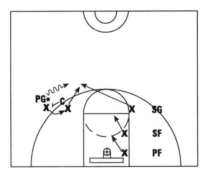

Drill #98: Pop-Out and Slide

Objective: To teach and practice the pop-out and slide switching techniques used in preventing the pick and roll.

Description: This two-on-two drill, involving any two offensive players and their defenders, can take place anywhere on the floor. The ballhandler is dribbling the ball, and his teammate moves over to set a screen. The screener's defender stays with him and bumps the screener as aggressively as he can get away with. As the ballhandler dribbles over the top of the screen, the screener's defender pops out and switches onto the dribbler, attempting to push him back to his original defender. The original defender moves quickly to the ballside of the screener to prevent the roll to the basket (Diagram A). One variation of the pop-out technique, the slide maneuver, is shown in Diagram B. Instead of trying to move the ballhandler back to the original defender, the screener's defender slides into position to prevent penetration into the lane.

Coaching Point:

* The coach should emphasize the timing of the pop-out maneuver and the importance of good communication between the defenders.

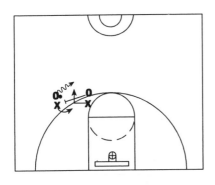

Diagram A

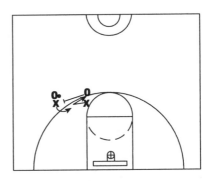

Diagram B

Drill #99: Screen Down "D"

Objective: To improve the defenders' abilities to deal with a situation where a player coming from a wing position screens down on the post.

Description: This drill is designed to deal with a specific situation that exists when the flow of play has left the power forward (PF) on the wing and the wing player (SG) down on the post. The point guard's (PG) defender forces PG to stay on the same side of the floor. The wing defender has been in a position to deny the pass to PF, and as PF moves to set the screen, the defender continues to bump PF's ballside shoulder to upset the timing of the play. The post defender has been in a deny position on SG, and when PF sets the screen, the post defender pops out and switches onto PF, staying high to deny the pass. The wing defender then reverses direction, picks up SG breaking out for the pass, and remains in a deny position. Diagram B shows how to defend the same downscreen if no mismatch exists. The two defenders use the same bumping techniques applied in disrupting any screen, but do not switch in order to keep PF down low. A team should not allow a size mismatch inside that puts them at a disadvantage.

Coaching Point:

- The coach may choose to encourage players to switch any time it will keep the bigger players down inside and leave the smaller players on the perimeter.

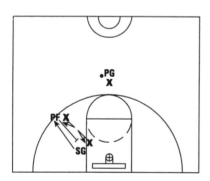

Diagram A

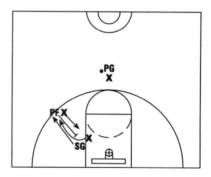

Diagram B

Drill #100: Defending the 1-4 Offense

Objective: To teach and practice defense against an offense in which only one point guard remains out front.

Description: The players should be positioned as shown in the diagram below. The defense has been inverted to keep the big players in low post defense. The point guard (PG) has the ball, and his defender's job is to keep the ball on one side of the court. If the shooting guard (SG) and small forward (SF) screen for each other on the baseline, the post defenders switch to defend against it. On down screens from the power forward (PF) to SG or the center (C) to SF, the screen-down defense described in Drill #99 is used. Players should attempt to switch any time it will leave the defense with their bigger players down inside. Defenders should use bump and trail options only if a switch will not work.

Coaching Points:

- The emphasis should be encouraged to play "physical defense".
- The defensive point guard should be taught never to allow the ball to be in the middle of the court, but to always force the dribble to one side.

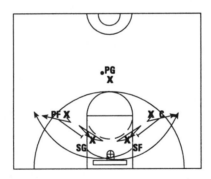

Drill #101: Post Cross-Screen Drill

Objective: To improve the post defenders' abilities to cope with cross-screens coming from one side of the low post to the other.

Description: This drill involves two low post offensive players and their defenders, positioned as shown in the diagram below. A wing player whose only function is to pass the ball to an open player is also needed. The ballside defender fronts his man to deny the pass to the ballside low post. The ballside post player breaks across the lane to set a screen for his teammate, and his defender lets the other defensive player know the screen is coming. The weakside defender moves above the screen to deny his man the opportunity to cut to the middle above the screen, and his teammate breaks off the other side of the screen to remove the baseline cut option. The weakside defender is also in position to switch to the ballside post player if he breaks back toward the ball for a pass after setting the screen. In that case, the ballside defender slides to the offside post position, and his teammate takes over the ballside defense. The drill continues with the offensive post players attempting to score any time they get a pass from the wing.

Coaching Point:

- The coach should emphasize the importance of good communication between the defenders.

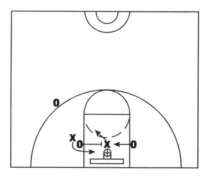

THE
AUTHORS

George Karl is the head coach of the Seattle SuperSonics. Since assuming his present position on January 23, 1992, Karl has led the Sonics to over 300 victories. In the process, Karl has the distinction of having achieved the highest winning percentage of any coach in Sonics histjory. Under Karl's tutelage, the Sonics have become one of the NBA's upper echelon teams. Twice, the Sonics have finished first in the NBA's Pacific Division, and in 1996, thay reached the NBA Finals. A 1973 graduate of North Carolina where he played three years for Dean Smith's Tar Heels and gained All-American honors as a senior, Karl began his distinguished coaching career in 1978 as an assistant in the ABA for the San Antonio Spurs. After two seasons with the Spurs, Karl then moved to the Continental Basketball Association as the head coach of the Montana Golden Nuggets. After three years with the Golden Nuggets, he began his NBA head coaching career with the Cleveland Cavaliers in 1984. Two years later, Karl accepted the same position with the Golden State Warriors—a job he held for two seasons. Subsequently, Karl spent two additional seasons each with the CBA's Albany Patroons and with Real Madrid of the Spanish League. One of the most respected and knowledgeable coaches in the game, Karl resides in the Seattle area with his wife Cathy and their two children—Kelci and Coby.

Terry Stotts is an assistant coach with the Seattle SuperSonics. He began his career with the Sonics in 1992 as a scout, before assuming his present position prior to the start of the 1993-94 season. In addition to his normal coaching duties, Stott's responsibilities include game preparation, coordinating NBA advance scouting, developing the Sonic defensive playbook and developing and coaching the Sonic forwards and centers. A 1980 graduate of the University of Oklahoma where he earned numerous honors as a basketball player for the Sooners, Stotts began his coaching career in 1990 as an assistant coach with the Albany Patroons under current Sonic head coach George Karl. He then spent one season as an assistant with the CBA's Fort Wayne Fury, before joining the Sonics staff. Terry and his wife Jan reside in the Seattle area.

Price Johnson is a successful youth basketball coach and basketball camp director in the Bellevue, Washington area. For the past 15 years, he has worked both as coach and as advocate of youth basketball. Since 1992, Johnson has taken an all-star youth basketball team to the national tournament for youth basketball, placing in the top 10 teams each year. Johnson has also done considerable volunteer work—serving on the Board of Directors of the Petaluma, California Boys and Girls Club working with the Boys and Girls Club of Bellevue, Washington and spending time assisting several high schools in the greater Seattle area. Johnson is a co-owner of Hoopaholics, a successful sportswear company. Price and his wife of 16 years, Julianne, reside in Bellevue, Washington with their two sons—James and Dane.

Terry Stotts, George Karl, Price Johnson (L-R)

ADDITIONAL BASKETBALL RESOURCES FROM

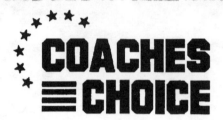

- **_101 OFFENSIVE BASKETBALL DRILLS_**
  by George Karl, Terry Stotts and Price Johnson
  1997 ▪ Paper ▪ 120 pp
  ISBN 1-57167-078-5 ▪ $15.00

- **_101 BASKETBALL REBOUNDING DRILLS_**
  by George Karl, Terry Stotts and Price Johnson
  1997 ▪ Paper ▪ 128 pp
  ISBN 1-57167-080-7 ▪ $15.00

- **_101 BASKETBALL OUT-OF-BOUNDS DRILLS_**
  by George Karl, Terry Stotts and Price Johnson
  1997 ▪ Paper ▪ 120 pp
  ISBN 1-57167-099-8 ▪ $15.00

- **_101 WOMEN'S BASKETBALL DRILLS_**
  by Theresa Grentz and Gary Miller
  1997 ▪ Paper ▪ 128 pp
  ISBN 1-57167-083-1 ▪ $15.00

- **_ATTACKING ZONE DEFENSES_**
  by John Kresse and Richard Jablonski
  1997 ▪ Paper ▪ 128 pp
  ISBN 1-57167-047-5 ▪ $15.00

TO PLACE YOUR ORDER:
U.S. customers call
TOLL FREE (800)327-5557,
or write
COACHES CHOICE Books, P.O. Box 647, Champaign, IL 61824-0647,
or FAX: (217) 359-5975